Acknowledgements:
The publishers wish to thank everybody who assisted in collecting the information and photographs contained in this book. Around the islands there were many people and organisations who gave their time and advice. In particular, we would like to thank Steve and Janet Simonsen for their help and friendship; Carol Lee; Janet Cook-Rutnik; Len and Nora Otley at Gallow's Point Hotel, the staff at Pavillions and Pools on St. Thomas and finally, to the people of the US Virgin islands for making our work on this guide such a delight.

First published by:
Morris Publications Limited, Cadogan Books
West End House, 3rd Floor, 11 Hills Place, London W1R 1AH, United Kingdom

In the USA by:
The Globe Pequot Press
PO Box 480, Guilford, Connecticut 06437-0888, United States of America

ISBN: 0-7627-0602-3
A catalogue record for this book is available from the British Library
Library of congress Cataloging-in-Publication data is available

Copyright © Indigo Books Limited 2000

All photographs by Steve Simonsen except for:
Debbie Gaiger: pages 1 (above left, below left, below centre); 14 (centre, centre right); 16 (centre); 18 (centre, centre right, below right); 2 21; 23 (centre); 26 (above right, centre right); 35 (right); 36 (right); 44 (below); 46; 51; 52; 61; 73; 88; 90 (right); 93; 96 (above right); 97; 98; 99 (left); 101; 108 (below right, below centre); 116 (above left, above right, below right); 118 (above); 119; 121; 128 (centre); 130 (centre); 134 (below left); 136.
Carol Lee: pages 23 (above) 30 (above, below); 31; 32; 33; 39; 56; 58; 60 (below); 62 (below); 63; 126 (above left, above right, below left) 128 (above, below); 134 (below); 141; 142; 143.
Janet Cook-Rutnik: pages 96 (above left, below right); 100, 102, 103, 104.
Mike Seale: page 53 (centre).

Designed by: RB Graphics, "Rickettswood", Norwood Hill, Horley, Surrey RH6 0ET United Kingdom.
Editors: Barbara Balletto and Debbie Gaiger
Proof-reading: Liz Sutherland

Printed and bound in China by Jade Productions

indigo guide to the us virgin islands

The Globe Pequot Press

Guilford, Connecticut

CADOGAN
island guides

London, England

nts

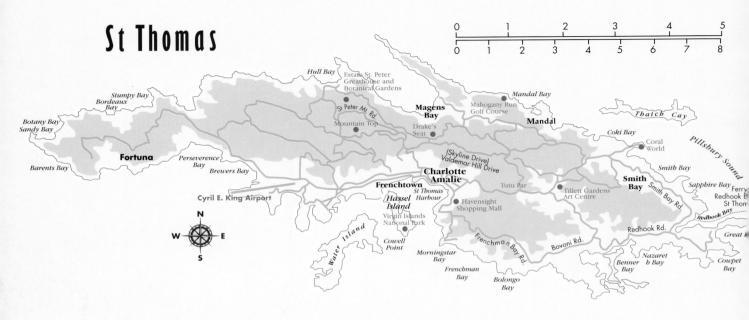

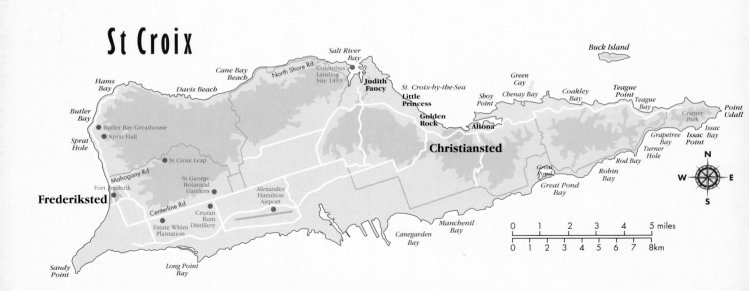

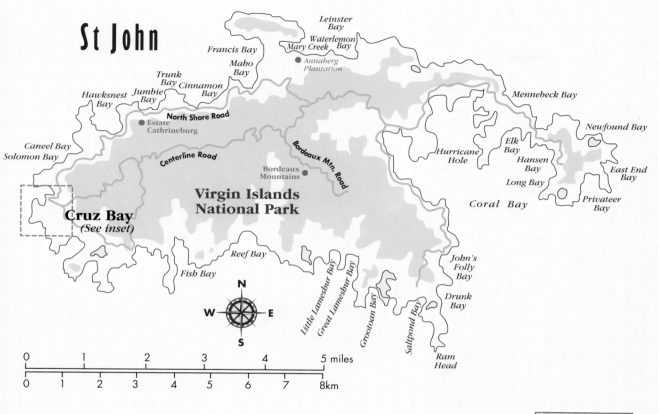

St John

Leinster Bay

Francis Bay

Waterlemon Bay
Mary Creek

● *Annaberg Plantation*

Maho Bay

Trunk Bay *Cinnamon Bay*

Mennebeck Bay

Hawksnest Bay *Jumbie Bay*

North Shore Road

Newfound Bay

● *Estate Cathrineburg*

Centerline Road

Elk Bay

Hurricane Hole

Hansen Bay

Caneel Bay
Solomon Bay

Bordeaux Mtn. Road

● *Bordeaux Mountains*

Long Bay

East End Bay

Virgin Islands National Park

Coral Bay

Privateer Bay

Cruz Bay
(See inset)

Reef Bay

John's Folly Bay

Fish Bay

Little Lameshur Bay

Great Lameshur Bay

Grootan Bay

Saltpond Bay

Drunk Bay

Ram Head

N
W   E
S

```
0        1        2        3        4        5 miles
0    1    2    3    4    5    6    7    8km
```

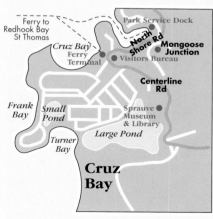

Ferry to Redhook Bay St Thomas

Park Service Dock

Cruz Bay Ferry Terminal

North Shore Rd

Mongoose Junction

● *Visitors Bureau*

Centerline Rd

Frank Bay

Small Pond

● *Sprauve Museum & Library*

Turner Bay

Large Pond

Cruz Bay

essential lists

lively places to get uncorked .

- Hotel 1829
- Virgillio's Wine Cellar
- Pusser's Pub
- Room with a View
- Morgan's Mango
- Alexander's Bar
- Duggan's Reef
- Dockside Pub
- Skinny Legs
- Greenhouse

great buys ...

- Duty-free perfume and cigars
- Fine art by the island's best artists
- Tapes or CDs of local musicians
- Colourful local t-shirts
- Local pottery
- Hand-made jewellery
- Duty-free electronics
- Fine cigars or liquers
- Arts and crafts including stained glass

lively places to eat ...

- Glady's Café
- Eunice's Terrace
- La Tapa
- Café Roma
- Indies
- Uncle Joe's Barbecue
- Sputnick's

great places to visit ...

- Charlotte Amalie
- St. Peter Greathouse and Garden on St. Thomas
- The Annaberg Plantation on St. John
- Coral World on St. Thomas
- The St. Croix Aquarium and Education Centre
- Buck Island off St. Croix
- Tillett Gardens on St. Thomas
- The Estate Whim Plantation on St. Croix
- The historic buildings in Christiansted
- St. George Botanical Garden on St. Croix

fabulous places to eat if money's no object ...

- Herve's
- Craig and Sally's
- Asolare
- Paradiso
- Hotel 1829
- Virgillio's
- Chateaux Bordeaux
- Top Hat

great beaches ...

- Trunk Bay
- Magen's Bay
- Maho Bay
- Coki Beach
- Sapphire Beach
- Cane Bay
- Hawks Nest Beach
- Cinnamon Bay Beach
- Waterlemon Beach
- Buck Island

great experiences ...

- A sunset cruise
- Sip a banana daquiri from the cocktail bar on Mountain Top, St. Thomas
- Snorkel in around the underwater trail on Buck Island
- Horseback ride along deserted beaches on St. Croix
- Join a hike through the magnificent rainforest
- Parasail above the beaches
- Take a trip on helicopter for a bird's-eye view of the Virgin Islands
- Watch the sun set from Sandy Point on St. Croix
- Scuba dive amidst some of the finest reefs in the Caribbean

.......the us virgi

sland experience

The US Virgin Islands is a tropical haven with miles of deserted palm-fringed white and beaches, crystal-clear aters and magnificent scenery. sitors quickly discover that ey are in an exotic, yet cognisably American, holiday estination. Yet, for all its miliarity to visitors from North merica, the US Virgin Islands e essentially West Indian. choes of the islands' European, frican and Caribbean heritage is rongly evident, reflected not nly in the people and language, ut also in the traditions, history nd cuisine.

olcanic, rugged and dramatic, e US Virgin Islands are located bout 70 miles (112 km) east of uerto Rico and 1,000 miles ,600 km) south-east of Florida. hey are made up of the three ain islands of St. Thomas, St. ohn and St. Croix, as well as pproximately 70 cays and islets, ost of which are uninhabited.

lthough English is the main nguage, it is spoken with a lilting Creole, or Calypso patois that differs slightly between the islands. In St. Croix, pockets of expatriate Puerto Ricans speak Spanish – an influence that has created a creolised dialect called Cruzan. Cruzan is, incidentally, also the name of St. Croix's famous export, rum.

The cultural distinctions between the three islands, as well as a chance to explore the nearby British Virgin Islands, make for endless sightseeing and recreational activities. The US Virgin Islands has carved out a reputation as one of the most varied destinations in the Caribbean. While the islands' beaches are quite magnificent, this is certainly not the only attraction on offer. Rainforests wait to be explored, along with botanical gardens, underwater marine parks, nature reserves and national parks.

The Danish, and to a lesser extent, the British, left a rich architectural legacy with buildings dating back at least 200 years. They range from the Classical Revival splendour of Government House in Charlotte Amalie to the shady Victorian arcades of Christiansted. The Danish heritage is still in evidence in some of the waterfront towns with their colourful warehouses and narrow alleys, as well as in the plantation windmills scattered around the countryside.

The US Virgin Islands is a paradise for sports enthusiasts with some of the world's finest big game fishing grounds for amateur and professional anglers. Over the last few years many world records have been broken, particularly for blue and white marlin. There is excellent year-round fishing for bonito, kingfish, sailfish, marlin, barracuda and wahoo. The blue marlin fishing season is best between July and October.

Below: Delicate butterfly sips nectar from one of the many species of cactus to be found on the islands.

r left: Bird's eye view of Henley Cay in the arkling turquoise waters off St. John. entre: The calm waters and white sands Maho Bay on St. John. Right: The elicate pink portulaca is a common garden ant found throughout the tropics. ottom: Golden sunrise over St. John.

The islands are particularly well placed to cater to the yachting fraternity, with regular racing events open to visitors. They also offer an opportunity for holidaymakers to experience an affordable vacation afloat. Charters are offered as either fully-crewed or bareboat – the name used to describe yacht rentals with no crew or provisioning provided.

Day sails aboard catamarans and power yachts are easily arranged through any of the tour operators on the islands or through your hotel. Most excursions will serve a fabulous lunch at a secluded anchorage with time allowed for snorkelling. For the more romantically inclined, how about an idyllic cruise sipping cocktails as the sun sets?

The warm waters, glorious skies and steady trade winds make for a windsurfer's paradise, while some of the world's finest underwater coral gardens offer sensational snorkelling or scuba

diving. Clear waters provide excellent visibility for shallow water dives or for exciting deep-water adventures.

The main shopping district of Charlotte Amalie on St. Thomas a labyrinth of duty-free shopping restaurants and art galleries. Some 400 stores carry jewellery electronic goods, crystal, linens and liquor. With no sales tax and some gentle negotiation, good deals can get even better. Situated adjacent to the cruise-ship dock is the Havensight Mall whose offerings will surely satisf even the most impassioned reta therapist. Similarly, Christianstec Market Square on St. Croix offer dozens of shops selling hand-made art and crafts, as well as a vast array of international goods

Alternatively, on St. John, indulg yourself at Mongoose Junction ir Cruz Bay where there are severa artisan shops and studios house within a pretty network of walkways and buildings fashione from coral stone and mahogany.

The US Virgin Islands is home to many painters and sculptors. Th landscape and flora provides a vibrant palette of colours and textures that only serve to inspi the talented artists who exhibit their works throughout the

Top: The lee of Little St. James Island provides safe diving and the shallows teem with yellow wrasse and damselfish. Centre: Unique arts and crafts are found in abundance at Mongoose Junction on St. John. Bottom: Yachts moored in the tranquil waters of Cruz Bay. Opposite: During Carnival, the islands explode into a kaleidoscopic blaze of colour.

lands. St. John is home to umerous artisans working in ilk-screen, shell art, coral, tained glass, wax, copper, ainted enamel and clay, as well s more traditional mediums like /atercolours, acrylics and oils.

or wildlife enthusiasts, the lands are no less rewarding. here are mangroves, salt ponds, eagrass beds and coral reefs; he aquatic eco-systems alone upport over a thousand plant nd animal species.

he islands provide a safe haven or many indigenous and nigrating birds, such as the aribbean martin, the parrot and he brown pelican. The npressive sight of a majestic ed-tailed hawk soaring on the hermals or a peregrine falcon ropping like a missile is quite xtraordinary. Lying on the nigratory route of the planet's argest animal, the humpback /hale can be commonly bserved offshore during the /inter months.

he cultural bonanza of the US irgin Islands can best be xperienced in the revelry and xuberance of the music and ance. Nightlife, especially on t. Thomas, is varied and vibrant. r, let the world of West Indian

dance and music come to you. Excellent entertainment is regularly arranged at many of the islands' hotels and resorts. For anyone fortunate enough to be here during one of the three main carnivals – the St. Thomas Carnival in April, the Fourth of July celebration, or the Crucian Christmas Festival – will be in for a very special treat.

St. Thomas' annual post-Easter Carnival is an incredible spectacle of colour and light. It draws on African customs and traditions, including drumming, dancing, the *baboula* and the exhibition of devils, *jumbies* (spirits or ghosts) and other figures through masquerades. The *moco jumbi*, a regular at many island festivals, is likely to be found towering above the crowds on stilts. Carnival also features masquerade parades, feasts, calypso contests, Quadrille dancing (which has its origins in Germany) and steel bands.

Carnival is a cultural adhesive that has bound the Caribbean people together for generations. It is popularly believed that wherever one finds more than a handful of Caribbean people – be it a tropical island or big city street – there is sure to be a *bacchanal*. However, carnival is

much more than a huge party. Reuniting families and friends, carnival represents a grand fète; it is a cultural birthright passed down through the generations, keeping tradition alive and expressing freedom through the fusion of music and dance.

And if Carnival is a sweet celebration of life itself, let the party begin!

Geography

The US Virgin Islands sit at the western end of the Lesser Antilles archipelago in the Anegada Passage, the channel that connects the Caribbean Sea and Atlantic Ocean. The Virgin Islands are actually peaks of submerged mountains, some of which are extinct volcanos, and cover an area of 140 square miles (360 sq km). St. Croix is the largest island covering an area of 82 square miles (213 sq km). It sits about 40 miles (64 km) south of St. Thomas and St. John. St. Thomas covers an area of 32 square miles (83 sq km), and St. John an area of about 20 square miles (52 sq km).

The People

The majority of the population is divided between the islands of St. Thomas and St. Croix, each of which have around 57,000 people. St. John has a population of about 3,500 people. The islanders are mainly descended

Photographs clockwise from top left: Sandy Point on St. Croix is the longest beach in the US Virgin Islands; calm warm waters provide perfect conditions for hard and soft corals; smiling youngster; the exquisite white sands of Trunk Bay on St. John; lone yacht moored in the calm waters off Maho Bay on St. John; the island's abundant flora adorns many roadsides in dazzling and varied shades.

from the slaves imported from Africa in the 1600s. There is also a confluence of nationalities from other Caribbean islands, as well as descendants from the early European settlers.

Most of the islanders are of the Catholic faith, although Anglican, Episcopal and Jewish denominations are represented. The Lutheran Church in Charlotte Amalie is the second oldest in the Western Hemisphere. The town is also home to the second oldest synagogue in the Americas.

History

Long before Columbus discovered the islands, the area was a major cultural centre for various Amerindian groups, including an Arawakian-speaking people known as the Igneri (many call them the Arawaks) from present-day Venezuela. They were adept potters, weavers, builders and agriculturists who sailed to the islands in dug-out canoes some 2,000 years ago.

By AD 200, these industrious people were established throughout many of the Caribbean islands. They enjoyed nearly 800 years of peace before they were overcome by the

Kalinago. The Kalinago, better known as the Carib Indians (a derogatory and untrue label conceived by Europeans to signify that these people were cannibals), were warriors by nature. They were also master mariners and fishermen and quickly dominated the pastoral Igneri, pushing them down the island chain as far as the Leewards.

By the time that Columbus arrived in 1493 on his second voyage to the New World, the Kalinago were the supreme rulers of the Greater Antilles.

Columbus landed in what is today known as Salt River Bay on the north coast of St. Croix. He named the island Santa Cruz (meaning Holy Cross) and, although his men were repelled by the Kalinago, he claimed the islands for Spain as part of the New World. Salt River was an important settlement and religious centre for the Amerindians and many historic artefacts have been unearthed in this area. Today, there is a marker near the beach commemorating the historic landing and in 1993 on the 500th anniversary of the Spanish arrival at Salt River, the landing site and surrounding land was declared a National Park.

Governor of Puerto Rico, Juan Ponce de Leon, concluded an agreement with the Kalinago at Salt River that they would stop attacking nearby Puerto Rico and embrace Christianity if the Puerto Ricans provided them with fresh produce. The Spanish broke their promise and started to use the islands as a ready source for Kalinago slave labour, whom they exported to the mines and plantations of Hispaniola – today, Puerto Rico, the Dominican Republic and Haiti. The Kalinago attacked Puerto Rico and in 1511 the King of Spain ordered that all Kalinago be killed. By the late 16th century the Kalinago had been virtually eliminated, either killed or enslaved. During the next hundred years, contrary to Spanish resistance, the Virgin Islands – bountiful in tobacco, cotton and sugar – were fought over and settled by the Dutch, the French and the English.

Columbus named the island chain Las Islas Virges (the Virgin Islands). It is reputed that as he sailed through the sea mist past the islands he was reminded of a painting depicting the Celtic princess, St. Ursula, and the 11,000 kneeling virgins who were massacred en route to Rome in the 4th century. In 1509, the

By the mid 1600s a number of settlements had been established on St. Thomas by small English, French and Dutch communities. However, on 30 March 1666, a Danish force led by Erik Smidt landed on the island and claimed it for the Danish crown. The Danes had arrived with few supplies and sent back urgent requests for provisions. Before these arrived, a Dutch force landed and deposed the Danes. The Dutch were ousted in 1672 when an expedition led by Jorgen Iverson landed from Copenhagen. He became the first Governor of the island and established a network of farms to supply Denmark with tobacco, cotton and sugar. The island was divided in plantations of 125 acres (50 hectares) each but the soil was poor and the terrain hilly which was quite unsuitable to any form of intensive farming.

Two years later, the first African slaves arrived in St. Thomas to work the sugar plantations and the island's prosperity began to develop. St. Thomas flourished as a centre of trade and commerce and became a stop-off point for ships travelling between the Caribbean islands and for those that had crossed the

lantic. It also became known as
centre of pirate activities,
cluding those of the notorious
ward "Blackbeard" Teach and
ptain William Kidd. Blackbeard
as a burly man with a thickly
atted beard which he braided
th blood and food. He terrified
s enemy who often believed
ey were being attacked by the
vil himself. The pirate ships
eyed upon the treasure-laden
lleons and would offload their
unty in the islands before
ending time ashore waiting for
eir next expedition. St. Thomas
ospered during the era of
acy and many of the
arehouses that still stand along
e waterfront were filled with
e rich pickings captured by the
ates. By the end of the 17th
ntury the British Admiral
enbow described St. Thomas as
"receptacle for thieves".

e Danes claimed St. John in
84 and finally settled it in 1717
en several settlers from St.
omas arrived with scores of
rican slaves to establish sugar
antations there. The slaves
ere subjected to appalling
eatment by their owners and
e new Governor introduced
ore stringent punishments for
sobedience, including
mputation, torture, floggings

and even death. The island had
been hit by a hurricane earlier in
the year and consequently food
supplies were scarce and many
slaves died of starvation. On 13
November 1733, the slave
population rebelled and attacked
Fort Frederiksvaern. Plantations
and mills were burned, Great
Houses were destroyed and
many white settlers massacred.
The slaves remained in control of
the island for six months despite
an unsuccessful attempt by the
British Navy to secure the island.

Finally a force of 400 soldiers
from Martinique surrounded the
slaves and the rebellion was over.
The leaders, however, refused to
surrender and jumped over the
cliffs to their death rather than
face the torture and execution
that awaited them.

*Opposite: The fabulous mosaic which
adorns the front wall of St. Ursula's Church
on St. John is the creation of artist Lisa
Crumrine. Below: The Catherineberg ruins
on St. John are just off the Centerline Road
on the way to Bordeaux Mountain. The
plantation was one of the first on the island.*

During this period, St. Croix endured much turbulence and unrest. By 1642, the Dutch had established a settlement on the north coast in what is now Christiansted, and the English were based on the west coast a Frederiksted. There were many disputes between the two nations, and in 1645 the Dutch Governor was assassinated by the English in a reprisal killing fo the murder of their own Govern The Dutch left the island and fo five years it remained in the hands of the English. In 1650, a force of 1,200 Spanish soldiers arrived from Puerto Rico and killed many of the English settlers. Despite this, and their successful rebuttal of a Dutch invasion, they were forced to surrender to the French a year later. Under the command of De Poincy, Governor of the French West Indies, the island was claimed by the French crown an sold to De Poincy in 1651. The island's name was changed to S Croix and the land was divided into plantations and townships. However, the colony did not flourish and in 1665 the island was sold back to the French We

Left: Memorable sunset over Cruz Bay on St. John. Centre: Statue in Frederiksted commemorating Emancipation. Right: The ecomony of St. Croix is an island of rich fertile land.

...ia Company. Nine years later, ...nership reverted to the French ...own. In 1733, St. Croix was ...rchased from the King of ...ance for 750,000 francs by the ...nish West India Company and ...e island's prosperity started to ...om. However, the company's ...licy began to strangle economic ...vancement and in 1754, on the ...ders of the King, St. Croix was ...clared the property of the ...nish Crown.

...the mid 1700s all the islands ...ere flourishing. St. John was ...st to massive sugar cane and ...tton plantations, and St. Croix

was the home of the Danish West Indies capital of Christiansted, as well as being an agricultural economic base. St. Thomas, with its free port status, remained a major slave and trade centre. The neutral status of the Danes protected the islands from the wars between Britain, France and Spain. In times of war they became a refuge against the brigands hired by the warring nations to harass their adversaries and in peace time they were the contraband headquarters of the area.

The British, who had objected to the Danish support of the American War of Independence despite their alleged neutrality, seized the islands twice – once in 1801 and again in 1807. In 1792, the Danes were the first nation to abolish the slave trade, although the ownership of slaves continued for many more years. In 1847, the Danish King Frederik VIII announced that slavery was to be abolished, but to ease the

repercussions this would have on the economy of the plantations, it was to be phased out over a period of 12 years and the slaves would not be truly emancipated until 1859. This announcement caused the slaves to revolt, and in an effort to avoid further periods of unrest Governor General Peter von Scholten was forced to defy the Crown and free all the slaves immediately. He was tried for negligence, but was later acquitted. The end of slavery saw the islands plummet into financial decline, with sugar crops failing and plantations being forced to close. The economic collapse of the islands spurred the Danish government into finding a way to get rid of this tropical burden. In 1866, the

United States showed interest in purchasing the islands for $7.5 million dollars. However, the move was rejected by the islanders, and it was not until 1917 that the secession was agreed and the three islands became an unincorporated territory of the United States for $25 million dollars. At that time there were very few roads on St. Thomas and no education beyond primary school, but the

Below: The calm clear waters of the Caribbean provide the perfect conditions for sailing enthusiasts.

Danish administrative structure was retained to ensure a smooth transition period. In 1927 an act was passed which granted the islanders citizenship of the United States. However, even today, Virgin Islanders are not permitted to vote in national elections.
From 1917 to 1931 the islands were administered by the US Navy because of their strategic position in the Caribbean on the passage to the Panama Canal. In 1931 the islands were placed in civil jurisdiction under the Department of the Interior and

the first civilian Governor, appointed by the President in consultation with the Senate, was sworn in. In 1970 this changed and the islanders now elect their own Governor and legislature. Two years later their first delegate, Ron de Lugo, was sent to the House of Representatives. The current Governor is Charles W. Turnbull.

In the early 1930s the Virgin Islands Company was created to develop the infrastructure of the island. The sugar industry was centralised and tax incentives offered to attract investors. A huge oil refinery was established in the mid 1960s by the Hess Oil Company and other light manufacturing businesses thrive today. The islands enjoy a comparatively high standard of living and low unemployment due largely to the tourism industry. The islands welcome some two million visitors per year, many of whom are day visitors on cruise ships or yachts.

ST. THOMAS

As the second largest of the US Virgins, St. Thomas embraces the wild Atlantic Ocean on its north side and the serene waters of the Caribbean Sea on the south. Spectacular scenery and

eathtaking views compete for ttention with a maze of stone-aved alleyways and innumerable uty-free boutiques. St. Thomas one of the most developed ands in the Caribbean. The apital of Charlotte Amalie – the ub and commercial centre of the rritory – bustles with vendors gainst an attractive backdrop of uropean architectural heritage.

onsidered to be the primary ruise ship stopover of choice in e Caribbean, St. Thomas eceives an almost daily influx of sitors and the harbour at harlotte Amalie is rarely quiet. n the eastern shores of St. homas, the village of Red Hook as prospered as the ferry ansfer point to St. John and has eveloped a sporty ambience of s own. Vacation hideaways of

every description blend into the verdant hillsides and dot the water's edge in secluded bays and coves.

St. Thomas is home to over 40 sandy beaches. Coki Beach is among the best and offers a wide selection of watersports, as well as excellent snorkelling and scuba diving. Coral World, which sits beside Coki Beach is a fabulous marine park with nature trails, turtle pools and an aviary. A popular windsurfing spot, and nominated by *National Geographic* magazine as "one of the three most beautiful beaches in the world", Magens Bay is the island's most popular beach. On the north coast, it is a magnificent mile-long strip of golden sand protected from the Atlantic by a narrow strip of land. For those looking for peace and quiet, charter a boat and sail to one of the dozens of uninhabited islands offshore and discover your own nirvana.

St. Thomas also offers interesting hiking tours of beach and wooded areas, as well as seasonal whale watches. Active

holidaymakers can easily fill their days with sightseeing and watersports, and their evenings dining at some of the finest restaurants in the Caribbean. An island of contrasts, St. Thomas offers many diversions – the choice is yours!

Left: View from Water Island looking towards the natural deep water harbour of Charlotte Amalie. Below: An exhilarating parasail ride is a fabulous way to enjoy a birds-eye perspective of the islands.

T. JOHN

rom its lush emerald mountains
o its sparkling turquoise waters,
t. John is a picture-perfect
ideaway for those looking to
scape from the crowds. Just a
0-minute ferry ride across the
illsbury Sound from the bustle
f St. Thomas, and situated on
he far west of the island, the
own of Cruz Bay is a fascinating
iosyncratic complex of colourful
hops and restaurants.
lternatively, the sunseeker will
e delighted to find that the
oast is lined with some of the
ost beautiful beaches in the
aribbean. The least populated,
nd unique in that nearly 70 per
ent of the land is managed by
he Virgin Islands National Park
ystem, St. John is the smallest
f the US Virgin Islands.

otal relaxation can be achieved
y strolling along exquisite,
owder-white sands fringed by
hady coconut palms punctuated
ith an occasional dip in the
rystal-clear sea. Alternataively,

*hotographs clockwise from top left: Trunk
ay on St. John was previously voted one
 the world's most beautiful beaches by
ational Geographic Magazine; vibrant
ougainvillea frames the doorway of a Cruz
ay store; wrought-iron bell in Hotel 1829
 St. Thomas; the waters off the east end
 St. Thomas have many uninhabited
oves and cays that can be explored by
yak; dazzling yellow tropical blooms.*

opt for a little more activity and
explore the parks, ruins and
nature trails. On St. John visitors
can horseback ride on the
beaches and discover flora typical
of a rainforest habitat, ancient
petroglyphs and old plantation
houses. Remnants of St. John's
plantation past are very much in
evidence along the trails. They
also take in many lovely bays,
rugged mountain forests, dry
cactus woodland and vantage
points that afford fantastic views
across to St. Thomas and the
British Virgin Islands.

Whether you succumb to the
island's luxurious resorts or
submerge yourself in its clear
waters for only a day, St. John
will undoubtedly capture your
imagination and affection.

ST. CROIX

Boasting the most diverse terrain
of the US Virgin Islands, from the
rugged mountain area of semi-
rainforest in the west to arid
hillsides that bloom with cactus
in the east, St. Croix offers
visitors a bountiful package of
dreams. Here, gently sloping hills,
roll down like seas of grass to the
coastal plains and disappear into
the ocean. The beaches are
uncrowded and fringed with
pristine coral reefs.

Set between the indigo blues of
sea and sky, the picturesque
harbour of Christiansted shelters
a town that is an architectural
showpiece and a Mecca for
shoppers. The attractive deep-
water harbour at Frederiksted
has the ambience of a town
steeped in history and is
characterised by pretty
gingerbread buildings, some of
which have been restored.

The hillsides of St. Croix are
scattered with stone sugar mills
and plantation houses that allow
visitors to step back into the
well-preserved past. The Estate
Whim Plantation, authentically
restored and furnished with
period pieces, is a superb
example of the glorious days of
plantation life. St. George Village
Botanical Garden is a small park
built on the ruins of an old sugar
cane plantation. Covering 17
fertile acres (7 hectares)
cultivated with native plants and
shrubbery, growing up around a
pre-Columbian settlement, the
garden provides the perfect
setting for the ruins of a 19th-
century rum factory.

St. Croix also offers the visitor
guided hiking tours which take in
ancient tropical forests, unique
wildlife, cascading waterfalls and
fascinating ruins.

ST THOMAS

Although relatively small, St. Thomas is an extremely hilly island, so a tour of only 10 miles (16 km) might take several hours to complete. However, the ridge of mountains that run from east to west and separate the Caribbean and Atlantic sides of St. Thomas present the visitor with some breathtaking and unforgettable views. The east side of St. Thomas has many major resorts and some fabulous beaches, while the northern side of the island is quieter with less traffic, and is extremely lush with magnificent flora. A good map will ensure you get the most from your visit.

One of the Caribbean's finest natural ports, the landlocked harbour town of Charlotte Amalie is the hub of St. Thomas. Of all the towns in the US Virgin Islands, Charlotte Amalie probably has the most to offer. It is a delightful historic town with red-roofed white buildings scattered across the hillsides that surround the bay. Its vast deep-water harbour plays host to over 1,000 cruise ships every year and is one of the most popular ports of call in the Caribbean.

pectacular

harlotte Amalie

y 1674, St. Thomas had merged as one of the largest lave trading centres in the West dies and in 1681 the town was fficially established by Governor smit, who ordered the building f four beer halls along its aterfront. The town was named ap Hus (meaning rum shop) and as home to fewer than 40 habitants living in a row of ouses on what is today Main treet. By 1716, there were over 0 houses and several ware- ouses along the waterfront. The ettlement continued to grow ntil, in 1804, a devastating fire wept through the town and zed many buildings to the round. The rebuilding process, owever, was swift and today the ty features many old buildings hat date back over 150 years, as ell as many that survived the equent fires and hurricanes that aused widespread devastation etween 1804 and 1837. The own was renamed in 1730 after he wife the Danish King Christian . The buildings reflect an eclectic rchitectural style influenced by he many nations that have made heir homes here. Delicate French ngerbread fretwork sits side-by- de with Dutch gabled-roofs and ry Spanish terraces. The narrow

cobbled streets are also evocative of the island's colonial heritage and – although the waterfront is now separated from the old warehouses that line the dock by a main road – the picturesque alleys of warehouses are bustling with trade as they have done for hundreds of years.

Ever since its colonisation, Charlotte Amalie has sheltered settlers, slave ships and marauding pirates – all of whom have left their mark on what is widely acknowledged to be the emporium of the West Indies.

Justifiably a National Historical Landmark, construction began on **Fort Christian** in 1672 and was completed in 1678. Its crenellated clock tower was added in 1784 during renovations. The earliest structure in town, the red brick masonry fort, which is one of five forts the Danes built across the islands, once commanded a strategic view over the harbour.

Left: Charlotte Amalie's vast natural deep water harbour plays host to over a thousand cruise ships every year. Below: The red brick Fort Christian was built in 1672 and the clock tower added in 1784.

During its 300-year history the fort has served many purposes. It once garrisoned troops; served as the Governor's residence; was a Lutheran church, a prison, police station and courts. A number of infamous brigands were tried and executed here. The dungeons now house the **Virgin Islands Museum**, which is open from Monday to Friday 9am to noon and 1pm to 5pm. Admission is free. It contains a fascinating collection of Amerindian artefacts, as well as post-Columbian exhibits. There are great views across the town from its battlements.

Originally built in 1874 as barracks for Danish troops, the bright-green Italian Renaissance-style **Legislature Building** once housed US Marines and served as a high school. The "Green Barn" – as it is known locally – was also the site of the historic transfer of ownership of the Danish West Indies to the United States. It became the Legislature in 1957 and the Senate Chambers are open to the public

Top: The mint green Legislature Building was where ownership of the Danish West Indies was transferred to the United States. Centre: The bright yellow Post Office is located at the eastern end of Main Street. Bottom: The Seven Arches Museum houses a fine collection of antiques.

between 8am and 5pm. A charming garden fronts the entrance and there are scenic views across to the harbour.

Emancipation Park is a shady retreat in which to relax and observe island life. It commemorates the 1848 abolition of slavery in the Danish West Indies and is a popular meeting place. The park features a bronze bust of the Danish King Christian IX and a replica of the US Liberty Bell. There is also a small gazebo that is occasionally used for concerts. This area is one of the best places in town to find a taxi.

Souvenir-hunters can stroll under a sea of bright umbrellas at the adjacent **Vendors' Plaza**, where merchants sell everything from African souvenirs and local art to leather goods and hand-made jewellery. Nearby, the handsome brick building that first served as the **Danish Customs House** now houses a street-level shopping arcade. On the opposite corner is the yellow **Post Office** which is officially known as Emancipation Garden Station. There are three statues honouring Virgin Islands scholars opposite the entrance.

Dominating the eastern end of Main Street and once the island's favourite place for gatherings, the

Greek Revival-style **Grand Hotel**, with its upper-storey pillared porticos, was built in 1840 and opened as the Commercial Hotel and Coffee House. At the end of the 19th century the upper floor was destroyed by a hurricane. Today, the building houses shops and offices, as well as the **Visitor's Hospitality Lounge**. There are rest rooms, a pay phone, a place to relax from the heat of the sun and a tourist information centre where books and magazines are available. It is run by volunteers, so do leave a donation. Opposite is the **Athenaeum**, which hosted writers such as Somerset Maugham who, reputedly drank here while writing *Of Human Bondage*.

In contrast, Gothic Revival is well-defined in the **Frederick Evangelical Lutheran Church**, which was built in 1793 – replacing two earlier churches built in 1750 and 1789. The present building was refitted in 1826 after being gutted by fire. It has a fine collection of ecclesiastical silver, a centuries-old chandelier and some interesting plaques.

The area around **Government Hill** has a number of historic buildings, including Government House, Hotel 1829, Crown House and Blackbeard's Castle.

Once an elegant residence, the imposing three-storey neo-Classical Revival-style **Government House** is notable for its detailed brickwork and exceptional wrought-iron veranda. It was built in 1867 for the Danish colonial council and is now the official residence of the Governor. The ground floor is open during the week for tours from Monday to Friday, 8am to 5pm, and admission is free. Its art collection is worthy of inspection and includes works by Camille Pissarro, Thomas Hart Benton and Gustave Courbet. There are also a number of murals in the lobby painted in the 1930s by Pepino Mangravatti.

To the east of Government House is a striking example of classic Danish West Indian architecture in the authentically restored 18th-century home that is now the **Seven Arches Museum**. There is a fine collection of antiques inside the house which is decorated with period furnishings. It is open Tuesday to Sunday, from 9am to 3pm. For refreshments, you might want to take a tall, cool glass of bush tea – the local term for herb tea – which is served in the charming courtyard.

Below: The Frederick Evangelical Lutheran Church was built in 1793 and today houses a fine collection of silver.

plans anyway, but incorporated the steps made from coloured bricks which came in ships as ballast from England and Denmark. At the summit of 99 Steps (which actually number over 100!) is the 18th-century West Indian-style **Crown House**, once the home of Peter von Scholten before he moved to St Croix as Governor. It is open from Monday to Saturday from 10am to 5pm and features many original furnishings, including a hand-carved four-poster bed.

The **Hotel 1829** was built (in 1829, of course!) for a prominent French merchant named Lavalette and represents one of St. Thomas' finest examples of 19th-century townhouse architecture. A steep set of stairs leads up to the brightly-coloured original stone and stucco building, which has accented decorative black wrought-iron gates. Now a National Historic Site, the first-floor terraces still feature original Moorish tiling.

Above: The 99 Steps connect Government Hill with Little Tower Street in Charlotte Amalie. Right: Blackbeard's Castle sits high above Government Hill and affords fantastic views over the harbour.

The dining terrace affords a magnificent view over the harbour (*see Eat Your Heart Out, page 129*).

To the east of Hotel 1829, the famous **99 Steps**, which connect Government Hill with Little Tower Street, are typical of the Danish step-streets that linked dwellings where hillsides were too steep for carriages. Charlotte Amalie was reputedly designed by a city planner in Denmark who failed to understand the topography of the island. The road builders proceeded with the

ackbeard's Castle above
overnment Hill has one of the
ost commanding views of
narlotte Amalie. It is now a hotel
imed after the infamous pirate
dward "Blackbeard" Teach. The
monic pirate reputedly lived
ere in the early 1700s and was
entually killed during a shoot-
it with the British off the coast
North Carolina in 1718. The
nical watch tower was built in
79 by a Dane, Charles
oggaert. The oldest structure in
e Virgin Islands, the tower is 30
et (9 metres) high and was one
the many look-outs built to
ert Fort Christian and the town
impending attack.

ie imposing Greek Revival style
atherineberg was built by
overnor Hans Henrik Borg as a
sidence in 1830. Down the hill,
Bakery Square one is greeted
the austere charm of the
utch Reformed Church. Its
story is crammed with incident.
was founded in 1744 and
irned down in 1804. Rebuilt 40
ars later, it was blown down in
95 by Hurricane Marilyn and
ouilt again in 1997. The
onochromatic cream-coloured
ill, which starkly contrasts with
e dark green of the shutters
id carpet, imparts a feeling of
renity and peace.

Erected in 1833, the **St. Thomas
Sephardic Synagogue** is the
second-oldest in the Western
Hemisphere and is a fine example
of Moorish architecture. The
congregation was formed in
1796, but the first two temples
were destroyed by fire. The
Jewish community was
established in St. Thomas by
Sephardic Jews fleeing the Dutch
island of St. Eustatius which had
been attacked by Admiral
Rodney during the American War
of Independence. Prominent
members of its congregation
have included Benjamin Franks

who led the incentive to oust
pirates from the islands; French
Impressionist painter Camille
Pissarro; author Herman Wouk;
Governor Ralph Paiewonsky and
the historian Isidor Paiewonsky.
The interior features rough stone
walls, white pillars and rich
mahogany benches. Sprinkled
with sand, the floor symbolises
the exodus from Egypt. The
Weibel Museum next door is a
showcase of Jewish history on
St. Thomas.

*Below: The St. Thomas Sephardic
Synagogue is the second-oldest in the
Western Hemisphere.*

Pause for a moment in **Rothschild Francis Market Square** which bustles with vendors selling exotic fruit and vegetables, fragrant herbs and freshly-squeezed juices. This is an excellent venue for a lunch-time snack. Additionally, the market has an extensive selection of African fabrics, artefacts and leisurewear for sale. In the 17th and 18th century as this was one of the busiest slave markets in the entire region; it is estimated that over a quarter of a million slaves were sold here before being shipped to plantations around the Caribbean and the United States.

The **Camille Pissarro Building** at 14 Main Street was the birthplace and residence of the acclaimed Impressionist artist. Nowadays it is home to the Caribbean Cultural Centre, comprising several shops and an art gallery. Members of the artist's family are buried in the Jewish Cemetery in St. Thomas and two of his paintings are on display in Government House.

Above: Rothschild Francis Market Square, sells exotic fruit and vegetables, fragrant herbs and freshly-squeezed juices.

The **Saints Peter and Paul Cathedral** dates back to 1848. The ceiling and walls are adorned with murals painted at the turn of the 20th century by artists from Belgium. The central altarpiece, carved from San Juan marble, features a beautifully rendered pastoral lamb. The side altars are carved with marble angels and winged cherubs.

By 1800, the island's expanding population led to the development of many simple wooden cottages to the west of Denmark Hill in Savan. Laid in a grid, this neighbourhood of small streets and dwellings became populated by freed slaves after the Emancipation in 1848. Savan is significant in that it remains an important comment on the island's social, historical and architectural history.

Interestingly, the warehouses that dominate the mid-town area were constructed of masonry that utilised any available material – stone, shells and brick were bound with a mortar made from sand and lime. When water was scarce, molasses was sometimes used. A series of devastating fires prompted the revision of building regulations that saw wooden roofs banned favour of tile and slate. Wide streets and courtyards were introduced, and many of the warehouses' 2-foot (half-a-metre) thick walls are original. After World War II they were converted into rows of attractive restaurants and shops. Those in search of duty-free bargains can now stroll the evocatively-named alleyways of Palm Passage, Royal Dane Mall and Creque's Alley.

Now the site of a hotel nestling at the top of Frederiksberg overlooking Charlotte Amalie, **Bluebeard's Castle** once

the 130-acre (32-hectare) Hassel Island is on the National Register of Historic Places.

Formerly a coaling and ship-repair station for the Royal Mail Steam Packet Company, most of the mile-long island is being developed as an historic and recreational area as part of the Virgin Islands National Park. Sights to see include the ruins of the Creque Marine Railway Complex, the Garrison House and Shipley's Guardhouse and Battery, as well as a rare example of a Napoleonic fort. Telephone 775-6238 or 776-6201, ext. 252 for information.

Frenchtown

Back in Charlotte Amalie, a short walk along the waterfront leads to Frenchtown, one of St. Thomas' best-kept secrets. Set apart from the rest of the island by its distinctive fishing village atmosphere, Frenchtown was settled in 1848 by emigres from the French island of St. Barthélémy (or St. Barths). Descended from the French Huguenots, they had fled mainland France to escape persecution from the Catholic authorities. They established a settlement near Gallows Hill and the community grew as more

immigrants arrived. In the mornings, brightly-coloured fishing boats reminiscent of 18th-century Normandy and Brittany bob up and down in the harbour and the fishermen clean and sell their catch beside the quay.

Left: Frenchtown on the outskirts of Charlotte Amalie is a small fishing community. Below Bluebeard's Castle which sits high above the harbour was used as a fort until 1735. Today, the grounds house a resort hotel.

arrisoned Danish troops, who sed its rounded tower as a okout. Armed with 11 cannons, served as a fort until 1735. oday, harbour views can be njoyed from the pool deck and fresco bar. The legend of the otorious pirate who murdered any of his wives has been omewhat embellished: the tower reputedly haunted by him and ome of his victims who met their eaths here.

assel Island

eparated from St. Thomas since 365, when Haulover Cut was edged to free the flow of water,

elegant to the rustic – all of which guarantee visitors a warm welcome. At the corner of Rue de St. Barthélémy, the Taste of Italy restaurant occupies what was once the site of St. Thomas' oldest saloon, Bar Normandie. Locals still speak with reverence of this beloved 1938 watering hole where regulars ordered libations through the shuttered side window.

The building across the Rue de St. Barthélémy intersection is reputed to be the original site of the Red Fox Inn, a notorious brothel during the days when pirate ships plied the waves. Today it is a grocery store.

Following Veterans Drive east from town leads to the West Indian Company Dock, where visitors can enjoy great views of the harbour and see the cruise ships close up. Sitting virtually in the shadow of these mammoth liners is the popular shopping Mecca of the **Havensight Mall** (see Shopping page 117).

Destroyed by Hurricane Hugo and rebuilt in 1994, the marina and retail complex on the boardwalk have been tastefully designed to complement the flavour of Frenchtown. A Caribbean version of New Orleans' French Quarter, there are many excellent restaurants and cosy bars to be discovered – ranging from the

Above: The cruise ship dock at Charlotte Amalie and Havensight Mall. Right: Tillett Gardens is an area of artists' studios, one of which produces unique stained glass.

Tillett Gardens

Once an old Danish cattle farm, Tillett Gardens, in the Tutu area of the island, was transformed by English silk-screen artist, Jim Tillett, into a peaceful sanctuary and a colony for local artisans. Visitors can wander here through this shady garden of stone walkways and watch a variety of artists at work in their studios. There is an art gallery, a goldsmith, a stained-glass studio, a candle-maker and silk-screen

udio. During the winter season tists from around the world erform at a month-long series of oncerts known as **Classics in the arden**. The **Arts Alive Fair** also kes place in October and is a ree-day showcase for local tists with live music and food. or information contact 775-1929 ee *Culture Club, page 97*).

ontinuing along the north coast, oth **Drake's Seat** and **Mountain op** offer unsurpassed views cross the island. Mountain Top, 550 feet (469 metres) above ea level, is a popular rest stop nd shopping area. The cocktail ar claims to be the original home the banana daiquiri – be sure savour one while taking in the credible views.

rake's Seat is reputed to be the ace that Sir Francis Drake used a look-out to watch his ships the harbour and to spot the panish Armada. There is a onderful view down to Magen's

Bay, particularly in the late afternoon when the sunset bursts into spectacular shades of vermillion, red and yellow. There is small market here and children can be photographed with a donkey decked out in colourful flower garlands.

Across from Havensight Mall is a prime vantage point for viewing both town and open sea. Sitting atop Flag Hill, **Paradise Point** provides a fine opportunity to relax and watch the sunset. Conveniently, visitors can reach

the 700-foot (213-metre) summit by taking the tramway. It operates throughout the day (Tel: 774-9809). At the top you can shop in one of the boutiques, hike the nature trail or relax on the deck with a refreshing beverage. Remember to bring your camera as the photo opportunities are unsurpassed.

Left: Drake's Seat overlooks Charlotte Amalie and is the legendary spot where Sir Francis Drake kept watch for enemy Spanish fleets. Below: The Paradise Point tramway transports visitors to the top of Flagg Hill in just five minutes and affords spectacular views over the harbour.

Atlantis Submarine

Cruise ship dock at Havensight Mall. Building No. 6, Bay L, St. Thomas

Telephone: 340-776-5650

Fax: 340-776-2919

Hours: 8am to 5pm. November to April, six dives a day, seven days a week. March to October four dives per day, four days a week. Telephone in advance for reservations and for schedules in the low season.

Entrance fee: US$72.00 per person, US$36.00 for children up to eighteen. Discounts for senior citizens.

Facilities: Due to restricted access and variable sea conditions, the company cannot carry passengers who are not able bodied.

The Atlantis Submarine and Harbour Cruise offers one of the island's most exciting tours. A unique and thrilling experience begins when you step aboard the *Atlantis III*, a state-of-the-art, air-conditioned passenger submarine. Designed and built in Canada, the 48-seat vessel transports visitors for nearly 2 miles (3.2 km) through the coral gardens of Buck Island, just outside Charlotte Amalie. The adventure begins with a scenic harbour tour followed by a 20-minute trip to the 65-foot (20 metre) Atlantis. It descends into the ocean depths not visible from the surface, offering spectacular views through the wide Plexiglas viewports that line each side of the hull. Passengers sit back-to-back in two rows close enough to the viewport to press their nose or camera against it. A co-pilot provides a running commentary on the corals, fish and other creatures that the submarine encounters on its journey. Classification charts for fish and coral are located inside the submarine and make for easy identification of the various species. Blue chromis, angelfish, parrotfish, yellowtail snapper and sea turtle are among the exotic creatures you will see swimming through the sea whips, brain coral and pillar coral. The vessel descends to 150 feet (45 metres) during the one-hour tour.

Left: A voyage on the Atlantis Submarine provides visitors with a close-up view of fabulous coral gardens. Above: The ghostly outline of the Atlantis Submarine.

The St. Peter Greathouse Estate and Garden

Off St. Peter Moutain Road (Route 40) heading north from Charlotte Amalie.

Telephone: 340-774-4999

Fax: 340-774-1723

Hours: 8.30am to 5pm

Entrance fee: US$8.00 per person with 25 per cent discount for senior citizens

Facilities: The grounds and observation decks are wheelchair accessible.

Perched high above the volcanic peaks of northern St. Thomas, the St. Peter Greathouse Estate and Garden was originally part of the plantation St. Peter built in the early 1800s. In 1938 the estate was sold to the appointed Governor of the US Virgin Islands, Lawrence W. Cramer, for US$400. Forty years later it was purchased to establish a botanical garden, but sadly hurricanes Hugo in 1989 and Marilyn in 1995 destroyed all the original buildings and gardens. The estate has since been rebuilt and transformed into a lavish retreat. Tours of the contemporary manor house, art gallery and 11-acre (4-hectare) tropical gardens

are available. The gardens are being re-established and contain over 180 species of tropical plants including cacti, waterplants and ornamental flowers. There are also over 100 varieties of exotic fruit trees. A self-guided nature trail leads through an orchid jungle to sparkling waterfalls and ornamental fishponds. Neighbouring islands and cays can be viewed from an observation deck 1,000 feet (305 metres) above sea level.

Below: The walkways around St. Peter Greathouse Estate. Right: Hanging heliconia is one of the many tropical plants to be found in the gardens.

Coral World

Located at Coki Point on the north east shore of St. Thomas

Telephone: 340-775-1555

Fax: 340-775-9068

e mail: www.coralworldvi.com

Hours: 9am to 5pm daily

Entrance Fee: Moderate; family passes are available for two adults and up to four children.

Facilities: Most of the park is accessible to people in wheelchairs. The Marine Gardens, Mangrove Lagoon, Turtle, Shark, Stingray and Touch pools are all accessible. The Caribbean Reef Encounter is partially wheelchair accessible; there are seven steps that bring visitors closer to the windows. The Underwater Observatory is only accessed by a spiral staircase and is therefore not wheelchair accessible.

Above: The Underwater Observatory at Coral World provides a fantastic opportunity to witness life on the coral reef. Centre: Hosts of French grunts can be seen from the Underwater Observatory at Coral World. Right: The Marine Gardens are a collection of twenty-one aquariums of dazzling natural seascapes which teem with colourful tropical fish and multi-hued corals.

Coral World is a beautifully landscaped 4.5-acre (1.5-hectare) marine park where the marine life and habitats of the Caribbean are displayed in fabulous underwater, outdoor and indoor exhibits.

In the **Underwater Observatory** you can experience a bewitching 360° view of a natural coral reef teeming with colourful tropical fish and other marine creatures. The observatory sits 100 feet (30 metres) offshore and is reached via a footbridge. The top level offers panoramic views of the surrounding islands and is a great place for spotting seabirds,

including brown pelicans, boobie frigate birds and laughing gulls. Stairs lead down to the 50,000-gallon (190,000-litre) **Predator Tank** which is home to sharks, moray eels, barracuda and othe denizens of the deep. A further set of stairs lead down to a roo that looks out onto the ocean floor and its fish, corals and underwater plants.

Other attractions include the **Caribbean Reef Encounter**, an 80,000-gallon (300,000-litre) tar filled with angelfish, grouper, Spanish hogfish, black durgons, spotted drums, lobster and sea enomes in an unrivalled etting of living corals and onges. Interpretive panels xplain the formation of coral efs and their role in supporting e marine environment. The **arine Gardens**, a dazzling ollection of 21 jewel-like tanks natural seascapes, present a ose-up view of tiny seahorses, orpionfish, yellowhead jawfish, oray and garden eels, uorescent corals and a clusive octopus. The **Turtle ool** is home to green sea rtles that hatched on Buck and National Monument off

the north shore of St. Croix in 1997. They were found buried in the sand by US Geological Survey biologists and flown to Coral World where they have received excellent care since. There are two feedings and talks each day at the Turtle Pool. There is also a **Stingray Pool** where regular feedings take place and a **Touch Pool** where visitors can gently handle starfish, sea cucumbers and sea urchins. Coral

World's knowledgeable staff will answer any questions about the park and its beautiful creatures, plants and trees. Lockers are available for US$3 per day so visitors can leave their valuables and sunbathe or snorkel at the adjacent Coki Beach. There is a dive shop open from 9am to 5pm, and visitors to Coral World receive a discount when renting snorkel equipment. There is a restaurant, bar and souvenir shop and the world's only underwater mailbox – which stamps postcards "Mailed Underwater at Coral World"!

ST JOHN

Pristine and remarkable, St. John's natural beauty has been thankfully preserved due to extensive donations of land to the US Federal Government back in the 1950s by philanthropist financier Laurance Rockefeller. Today, over two-thirds of the island is part of the Virgin Islands National Park and it remains wonderfully undeveloped.

The emphasis is on the outdoors and there are many fascinating trails to explore amid the island's steep overgrown hillsides. The coastline is dotted with stunning beaches and the underwater life is unsurpassed. The choice of accommodation is enormous, ranging from elegant five-star resorts, luxury villas and apartments to environment-friendly eco-camp grounds.

St. John is an absolute breeze to explore. One road runs along the north shore, another across the centre of the island. The roads are well maintained, albeit extremely hilly, with some unexpected precipitous curves and bends. Incredible drives lead through dense forest, across verdant hillsides and over cool mountain tops before ending back on the shimmering coastline. If you are planning a round-island tour, renting a car – whether an open-air jeep or a conventional vehicle – is more cost-effective and allows greater freedom than relying on taxis. There are plenty of reputable car-hire companies in Cruz Bay (See *Nitty Gritty, page 150*).

Alternatively, Virgin Island transit buses travel regularly between Cruz Bay and Salt Pond and charge US$1.00 for any stop on route. They follow the Centerline Road to Coral Bay and then continue to the terminus at the end of Salt Pond Road. Although there are a few official stops along the route, buses will usua pick up anybody who waves them down.

Situated in a picturesque harbou at the west end of the island, Cruz Bay is a charming example of a West Indian waterfront tow painted in bright primary colours During the day it bustles with activity and there are many interesting shops, numerous lively bars and a wealth of fabulous restaurants.

of this great Russian tenor who lived the last 40 years of his life on St. John until he died in 1995. Antique photographs and books are on display. It is open from Monday to Saturday from 9am to 11am and 4pm to 6pm.

Left: The shimmering crescent of Turtle Bay on St. John is lapped by warm turquoise waters. Centre: Full moon over the pretty town of Cruz Bay. Below: Ancient cannon at Fortsberg at the east end of St. John.

o enhance your visit here, the taff at the National Park Visitor entre in Cruz Bay are extremely elpful. The centre provides a election of maps and brochures nd also sells some interesting ooks on the region. Nearby, the **irgin Islands Communications entre**, Connections (Tel: 776-922), will arrange anything from inner reservations to sailing xcursions, deep-sea fishing trips r Internet access. It is run by hree women who give objective dvice for a small referral fee. onnections is also the local ecipient for national and ternational courier packages.

here are two worthwhile istorical attractions in Cruz Bay – **the Elaine Ione Sprauve Library and Museum** and the **Ivan Jadan Museum**. The former was built as a Great House in 1757 and today houses a library and museum displaying a collection of artefacts dating from ancient times. There are exhibits on the history of the Virgin Islands including some rare antique photographs. It hosts regular exhibitions of works by local artisans and it is open from 9am to 5pm Monday to Friday. Telephone 776-6359.

The Ivan Jadan Museum was created by the widow

The Annaberg Plantation

Telephone: 340-776-6201 ext. 238

Fax: 340-693-8811

Hours: 8.30am to 4pm

Entrance Fee: US$4.00

Facilities: The trails that lead to the ruins are wheelchair accessible, however some assistance is required.

The 500-acre (200-hectare) Annaberg Plantation fronts Leinster Bay and makes for a memorable stop on the road to Coral Bay. Built in the 1780s, this well-preserved plantation was once an important Danish sugar estate. The National Parks Service lead regular guided tours through the ruins. They also offer an informative brochure to accompany the self-guided trail, which explains the methods used in sugar processing and the function of different buildings.

Steps and wooden boardwalks lead from the parking area through a small forest to a paved trail around the plantation ruins. There is a windmill tower, slaves' quarters, boiling rooms and a still. Craft demonstrations are Periodically conducted by local residents and are a good way to learn how the islands' early inhabitants earned a living making charcoal, terracing gardens, weaving baskets and how they healed mind, body and soul with local plants and herbs. The estate affords sensational views across the Sir Francis Drake Passage to neighbouring Tortola and Jost van Dyke. From Annaberg follow the road up to

Left: Colombo's Café on the road from the Annaberg Plantation to Coral Bay. Above: The ruins at the Annaberg Plantation on the north coast of St. John.

enterline Road (Route 10) and top at **Colombo's Café** – an old an with its wheels buried in the and. This is a great place to top and sample the non- lcoholic fruit drinks which are uite delicious.

oral Bay is definitely a place to scape from reality. This tranquil, go-barefoot" community at the ry, eastern end of the island is asy-going and very laid back. It /as the first area settled by the anes and the dilapidated fort on he point dates back to the early 700s. Serious exploration in this area will require a jeep, as some of the roads are unpaved – however, a conventional car is fine if you are just coming for lunch.

From Coral Bay, Centerline Road carves a path up toward **Bordeaux Mountain**. At 1,277 feet (389 metres), it is St. John's highest peak. A natural catchment for showers, the luxuriant rainforest abounds with stands of

bay trees, the leaves of which are crushed to extract the oil used in the production of Bay Rum cologne. There are stunning views from Coral Bay Overlook of the islands to the north-east towards Virgin Gorda. Perched atop Bordeaux Mountain, **Le Chateau de Bordeaux** offers a special dining experience in an enchanting setting. (*See Eat Your Heart Out, page 131*).

Left: Bordeaux Mountain offers fantastic views over St. John and the British Virgin Islands. Above: Organic fruit and vegetables are grown on farms around St. John.

Trails

There are over 20 well-maintained trails that traverse St. John's 13,000-acre (5,200-hectare) National Park, which range from an easy 30-minute stroll through shady woodland to a strenuous half-day hike through mountain forest past historic plantation ruins down to a deserted beach. The **National Park Visitor Centre** produces a comprehensive trail guide and organises guided tours on certain days and their knowledgeable guides provide a wealth of information on the island's history, flora and fauna. It is advisable to make reservations well in advance as hikes quickly become booked up. Telephone: 776-6201 for information.

Always plan your hike with a map and notify friends where you are

going and when you plan to return. Never hike alone and give ample time to allow for uphill terrain, rests, exploring and swimming. Remember, this is the tropics, so carry plenty of water (none is available on the trails) and wear loose comfortable clothing. It is advisable to wear long trousers and a shirt to protect against sunburn and insects and carry a swimsuit and towel. Closed shoes or hiking boots are recommended for some of the steeper walks.

The **Cinnamon Bay Loop Trail** takes about an hour to complete. It offers shady respite

from the tropical sun and starts at the ruins of the **Cinnamon Bay Plantation**. The trail leads past an old Danish cemetery where Ann Margarethe Hjardemaal, the wife of a plantation owner, was buried in 1836. Continue through the forest where towering trees dwarf strangler figs, mango and bay rum trees. It is possible to catch the occasional sighting of geckos, tree lizards or a mongoose as it scampers through the undergrowth. Signs

Above: The Cinnamon Bay Loop Trail leads through cool shady forest on an easy hike which takes about thirty minutes to complete. Left: The trail leads past the cemetery where the wife of a Danish plantation owner was buried in 1836 – the inscription reads "Remember her with love"

ong the route provide
scinating information on the
egetation and historical sites.

he energetic can also tackle the
nnamon Bay Trail from the
ins along an old plantation road
the mountainside to Centerline
oad. It leads almost directly
ohill for one hour and takes in
me interesting flora and
rdlife. Most hikers, however,
efer the easier option: to start
Centerline Road and walk
own to North Shore Road. At
nnamon Bay Beach, which is
perated by the National Parks
ervice, there is an on-going
chaeological dig. Volunteers
ork under the guidance of
sident archaeologists in the
xcavation of an ancient Taino
remonial site. The pottery that
as been unearthed here dates
ack over a thousand years.

e Ram Head Trail

is popular two-hour trail is
njoyable, generally quiet and
asy. It begins at the southern
d of Salt Pond Bay and rises at
gentle pace over an arid
ndscape of Turk's cap cacti and
ntury plants before dropping
own to the stone-covered Ram
ead Beach. This hike is popular
ith locals on a full moon, but be
reful as it incorporates the

cactus-covered **Ram Head Point**,
some 200 feet (65 metres)
above the crashing surf. It is
essential to watch your footing
near the cliff edge at all times.
The views of Salt Pond Bay and
the British Virgin Islands are
fantastic, and on clear days it is
often possible to see St. Croix in
the distance.

For anybody interested in horse-
or donkey-back trail riding around
the hills and beaches of Coral
Bay, then look no further than
Carolina Corral (Telephone: 693-
5778). Run by the lovely Dana
Bishop, the corral offers riding on
tamed donkeys and horses
rescued from lives of neglect

around the islands. The rides
include the **Johnny Horn Trail**
which takes about one hour and
affords magnificent views over
Hurricane Hole from its summit.
Half-day, as well as sunset or full-
moon rides, are also available at
a cost of between US$45-90.
Dana's partner, Jeff, who
originally hails from Colorado,
divides his time between
escorting the rides, giving
lessons and assisting with the
upkeep of trails which have
become impassable because of
hurricane damage to the
vegetation and trees.

*Below: The precipitous cliff edge of Ram
Head point.*

The Reef Bay Trail

The **Reef Bay Trail** starts from Centerline Road, a short distance west of Bordeaux Mountain Road, and is a strenuous half-day hike. A 3-mile (5-km) walk downhill along an old Danish path leads to some well-preserved petroglyphs, two waterfalls, an abandoned sugar plantation, the Reef Bay Great House and eventually to Reef Bay. The National Park Service lead regular hikes for a maximum of 37 people along this trail.

It passes through a variety of natural habitats including a tropical forest dense with mango, lime and bay rum trees, century plants, cacti and vast root-buttressed kapoks. During the rainy season the area is blanketed with a profusion of spectacular wildflowers. Along the route, which eventually leads down to the scrub brush of Reef Bay, there are informative signs identifying the wildlife and flora in the area.

Halfway along the trail you reach the ruins of Par Force Village, the masonry walls being the only surviving evidence of the old plantation. From here continue along a dry river bed for five minutes to the **Petroglyph Trail**. A short walk alongside a 6-foot (2-metre) stone wall leads to a sparkling waterfall with a clear pool below where the petroglyph are carved into the rocks. Opinions about the origin of the petroglyphs are divided; some favour the Arawaks or Kalinago, others claim slaves of Ashanti ancestry are responsible. At certain times of year freshwater shrimp and crayfish can be seen in the waters while dragonflies da about the surface. A steep path to the left of the po leads to another waterfall and pool, but it is a strenuous climb and not encourage by the Parks Servic

Returning to the Reef Bay Trail, it is a short distan to the ruins of the **Reef Bay Mill** which operated as the last working sugar mill on the island until the middle of the 20th century. The ruins of the boiling house, grinding mill and distillery still stand – a testimony to the

quarters, stable and an outhouse. Until recently, the National Parks Service had been restoring this imposing building, but due to the vast expense involved, the project was subsequently abandoned.

There are many other fascinating trails to hike on St. John, including the **Bordeaux Mountain Trail**, the **Lameshur Bay Trail** and the **Lind Point Trail**. The National Park Service gives advice on the condition of each trail and the degree of fitness required.

Opposite: The waterfall on the Reef Bay Trail provides a cool area to rest during the hike. Centre: Along the trail hikers will encounter many fantastic species of flora, including the colourful ixora. Above and below: Ancient petroglyphs on the Reef Bay Trail.

and's bygone days of colonial andeur. The beach at Reef Bay a welcoming sight and you can her cool off here, or walk back the trail a short distance to other trail leading off to the left. short walk over a hill leads to a mpletely deserted sandy beach the other side of the bay.

sitors who join the Park Service ur will be ferried back to Cruz ay by small boat. Alternatively, you have tackled the trail under ur own steam, the only way ck is up!

turning up the trail affords you e opportunity to take a detour the **Reef Bay Great House**. To d it, look for the Lameshur Bay

Trail which heads east from the Reef Bay Trail just before the Petroglyph Trail. Follow this for about 300 feet (100 metres) and take the first turning on the left. The last working plantation before it ceased production in 1920, the Reef Bay Great House is the most architecturally ambitious structure on St. John. Its classical beauty is still very much in evidence and includes the remnants of a cook house, servants'

ST CROIX

St. Croix is the largest of the US Virgin Islands and is topo-graphically very different to St. Thomas and St. John. Vast stretches of agricultural flat land make up the dry eastern end of the island, while the mountainous western end supports a semi-tropical rainforest that receives up to 55 inches (140 cm) of rainfall per year. The land in the centre consists of fertile rolling hills largely devoted to farming.

St. Croix has many fine examples of colonial architecture and at the height of its prosperity was home to over 100 plantaton houses and sugar mills.

Although tourism is the main source of income for St. Croix, it is not over-developed and one can easily find empty beaches, quiet towns and a relaxed, friendly attitude amongst the local people. Visitors will be rewarded with an enriching holiday experience unlike that found on either of the other US Virgin Islands.

The island is a confluence of nationalities that include the original Cruzans, who are descended from the African

slaves, as well as large pockets of Puerto Ricans who moved here in search of a better life.

Sadly, 90 per cent of the island was devastated in 1989 by Hurricane Hugo, causing many islanders to lose their homes. Many of the historic buildings fortunately escaped serious damaged, but Hurricane Marilyn swept through in 1995 and wreaked further havoc.

St. Croix is best explored in sections, perhaps book-ending one's visit with a walking tour of Christiansted and Frederiksted at either end of the island.

Conveniently, an air-conditioned bus service operates between the two towns. Outlying areas can be toured independently by car or as part of a guided tour. For hikers, the St. Croix Environmental Association offer hikes through several of the island's ecological treasures, including Estate Mt. Washington Butler Bay, the Caledonia Valley and Salt River Natonal Park.

Above: Snorkellers explore the shallow ree just off Christiansted at Protestant Cay. Opposite: Fort Christianvaern is the best preserved of five forts built by the Danes. was built in 1749 and troops were stationed there until 1878.

Christiansted

ith pastel-hued architecture nd arcaded shops confirming its putation as one of the most cturesque towns in the aribbean, historic Christiansted estles between a busy harbour otected by offshore reefs and erdant hillsides. The town flects many fine examples of 8th-century architecture largely ue to the fact that it suffered wer fires than Frederiksted, or harlotte Amalie on St. Thomas. he town was laid out by the anes when they arrived in 1733 nd was named in honour of their ng Christian VI. It prospered ntil the collapse of the sugar dustry in the mid-1800s. By 948 the entire island and its chitectural heritage was xtremely run-down, but the rmation of the Landmarks ociety heralded the start of an tiative to maintain and restore any of the island's properties. he waterfront and town square as established as a **National storic Site** in 1952 and today is aintained by the National Park ervice. The main shopping reets are just behind the aterfront around King Street nd King's Alley. There are some xcellent duty-free bargains to be

found, as well as a fine selection of local arts and crafts, in a relaxed, low-key setting.

The best-preserved of all the Danish forts still standing in the entire West Indies, **Fort Christiansvaern's** four-pointed citadel is a prime example of colonial military architecture. Built around a square courtyard, its ramparts contain corner bastions and dank dungeons. Fashioned from yellow Danish brick, it took 11 years to build in the mid-18th century and was completed in 1749. Although the fort never saw action, troops

were stationed there until 1878, and it still displays an impressive arsenal of weapons which date back to the late 1600s. It was the guardian of the first successful French settlement on St. Croix. The fort is open from Monday to Friday 8am to 5pm and at weekends between 9am and 5pm. There is an informative leaflet provided by the National Park Service that gives details on a self-guided tour.

Across from the fort and built during the same period, a Georgian spire draws the eye to the fine rectangular design of

St. John's first Lutheran church, the **Steeple Building**. The building, which sits between Church and Hospital streets, was completed in 1753 and the Georgian steeple added at the end of the 18th century. Later utilised by the Danes as a military bakery, hospital and a school, it has been restored to its former glory. It now houses the National Park Museum and contains exhibits on the Arawak and Carib

Above: The Steeple Building in Christiansted was completed in 1753,

Indian settlers. The display includes part of the late Folmer Andersen's Arawak artefacts collection; an avid amateur archaeologist, Andersen served as the Director of the St. Croix Sugar Factory from 1916 to 1931 and devoted all his spare time to the discovery of these historical items. There are also archaeological displays on plantation life, antique maps and an exhibit on the architectural development of Christiansted. It is open from Monday to Friday from 9am to 4pm.

The church of the Dutch Reformed congregation, the **Christiansted Lutheran Church**, was constructed before 1740. The flooring, pulpit and gravestones which are now set into the walls, were salvaged from the Steeple Building when it was a place of worship. The Gothic Revival tower features excellent detail, while the older sections exhibit elements of Dutch Renaissance architecture.

At the intersection of Queen Cross and King Street, **Government House** is a fine specimen of colonial architecture. Constructed in 1747 as two

private homes, it is approached up an impressive staircase which narrows to an arch that bears the date 1830 and a Danish crown. The main hall contains a fine collection of furniture donated by the Danish Government in 1966. There is also a stately ballroom and traditional kitchen. In mid-1999, the building underwent extensive restoration and today houses the government offices and the court. Outside, an arched iron gate leads to a maze of European-style gardens.

Apothecary Hall stands on the site of an 1826 pharmacy set up by Danish pharmacist, Peter Eggert Benzon. He started his business in order to supply the medical needs of the garrison at Fort Christiansvaern and proved to be such a good businessman that he soon held the monopoly for pharmaceutical items across the entire island.

The **Post Office and Danish Customs House** dates back to 1734, although various extensions were subsequently added. It was the town library from 1927, and today it serves as the National Park Service Visitor's Centre and an art gallery. The old headquarters of the **Danish West India and**

uinea Company is now home to e police headquarters and the ost Office. Behind is a small ourtyard where slave auctions sed to take place. Today it is the te of a small farmers' market elling a variety of fresh produce.

ther good examples of Danish chitecture can be seen in Hill reet and East Street. The main opping area is around King treet where there are many ady alleys and narrow streets explore. The shopping here is xcellent and includes a wide riety of interesting stores.

e **Florence A. Williams Library** also on King Street and has an xcellent collection of books on e Caribbean and St. Croix.

e **St. Croix Environmental ssociation** is based in oothecary Courtyard (Tel: 773-989) and organises nature hikes different parts of the island, cluding Salt River National Park, state Mt. Washington and the aledonian Rainforest.

ey use the services of guides ho work independently, and clude experts on the island's ative flora and fauna. Each hike sts up to three hours and offers fascinating insight into the atural wonders that St. Croix as to offer.

St. Croix Aquarium and Education Centre

In the Caravelle Arcade in the centre of Christiansted.

Telephone: 340-773-8995

Fax: 340-773-8995

Hours: Open from Tuesday to Saturday, 11am to 4pm.

Entrance Fee: US$4.50 for adults and US$2.00 for children under 12.

Facilities: The centre is wheelchair accessible with some lifting up a small step.

Run as a non-profit educational centre, visitors are guided along a series of small aquariums containing a variety of marine life, including turtles, lobster and colourful reef fish. The tour lasts for 30 minutes, during which time visitors learn all about the feeding and mating habits of the fish, the names for the coral and the structure of the various marine habitats which exist on the island. There is a touch tank at the end of the tour where you can hold starfish, sea cucumbers and sea eggs.

Right: The St. Croix Aquarium and Education Centre incorporates a series of small aquariums that contain a diverse array of marine life.

Buck Island

Charter boats regularly ply across to the 880-acre (396-hectare) Buck Island National Monument, which sits 6 miles (10 km) off Christiansted. It rises to 340 feet (104 metres) and includes 704 acres (285 hectares) of water and coral reef systems. The area was first protected in 1948 and proclaimed a National Monument in 1961. Endangered species nesting here include the brown pelican, hawksbill, leatherback and green sea turtles.

Two-thirds of the island is surrounded by an elkhorn coral reef that includes a marine garden area which is closed to fishing activities. The underwater trail with interpretive signs lies off the eastern end of the island and is perfect for snorkellers looking to meander through coral grottoes and undersea canyons. The area teems with hundreds of multi-coloured tropical fish, including parrotfish, French angelfish and blue tangs.

There is an easy hiking trail to the island's highest point where you will be met by a spectacular vista of the reef below and the outline of St. John on the northern horizon.

Various concessionaires operate out to Buck Island including **"Captain Heinz"**, who is based in Green Cay Marina. He can be contacted on 773-3161 and transports passengers on his 42-foot (13-metre) trimaran.

Dive St. Croix, based in Christiansted, operate a variety of excursions over to Buck Island ranging from half-day trips on power boats to full-day trips on a sail boat. The cost typically ranges from US$35-55 for adults and US$25-35 for children. They also run scuba diving trips over to the island (Tel: 773-3434).

Exploring the East and South

Heading east from Christiansted towards the south coast, Route 82 leads through some prime real estate and past various ruins of old sugar estates. Passing St. Croix's oldest hostelry, which was built by the Knights of Malta, the 350-acre (140-hectare) Buccaneer Hotel offers wonderful views of the northern seascape (see Where to Hang Your Hat, page 142) . There are some

Above: Buck Island National Monument si just off the north coast of St. Croix and provides snorkellers with some excellent sightings of fabulous reef fish.

retty beaches all along this
oast, which eventually leads to
eague Bay, an ideal anchorage
or boaters visiting the St. Croix
oat Club. It is also a fantastic
oot for windsurfers and beach-
vers. The lowland area further
ong is home to **Cramer Park**, a
opular place for picnics and a
eautiful northern shore beach.
t weekends, the park is
ansformed into an outdoor
arty atmosphere with live music
nd DJs.

t the more arid easternmost tip
f St. Croix, the rocky
romontory of **Point Udall** can be
ther hiked or explored with a
ur-wheel-drive vehicle. The
imb, via a rutted dirt road, is a
tle slow-going but certainly
orthwhile for its magnificent
ews. This most eastern point of
ne United States is carpeted
ith wildflowers and cacti at
ertain times of the year. From
ere the Isaac Bay Trail leads to
n isolated beach protected by a
oral reef. The area offers good
norkelling in calm waters. A
nort distance from Point Udall,
e **National Science Foundation**
as funded the installation of a
ant five-million-dollar antenna
nat is 82 feet (25 metres) in
ameter. This 260-ton dish is
sed to explore the mysteries of

the universe and, when linked up
with nine other identical dishes
around the US, creates the
world's largest integrated
astronomical instrument and its
most powerful radio telescope.

Returning from Point Udall, look
up to see a curious architectural
hybrid of a Moorish mosque and
Agra's Taj Mahal. "**The Castle**"
was built by a recluse known as
Contessa Faber.

Along the south coast (Route 62)
there are various empty
beaches, including the white,
sandy **Grapetree Beach**,
where the Divi Resort has
recently undergone extensive
renovations to repair the
damage caused by Hurricane
Hugo. Further along is **Great
Salt Pond Bay** – an area of
salt flats and ponds that is a
delight for bird-watching
enthusiasts. The vegetation
is stunted and sparse along
the entire southern stretch of
coastline, but there are some
interesting trails to explore.
At the junction with Route 85
turn right and head back to
Christiansted to explore the
western, more tropical end of
the island.

*Right: Cane Bay Wall provides some
world-class diving opportunities.*

Exploring the West

The road heading west out of
Christiansted leads to St. Croix-
by-the-Sea and a section of
beautiful coastline. There are a
number of old estates along this
stretch, including places like Little
Princesse and Golden Rock.
There is an off-shore reef which
is a popular snorkelling site. A
right turn off Route 75 onto the
751 leads to the upscale
neighbourhood of **Judith's Fancy**
and the ruins of the largest

plantation on the island – a 250-year-old Danish Great House and tower. The "Judith" pays homage to Judith Heyliger, who was born in 1672 and is buried on the estate. It was built in the mid-1600s by Governor du Bois and became the headquarters of the Governor of the Knights of Malta.

At Hamilton Drive the road overlooks **Salt River National Park**, the location where Christopher Columbus anchored in 1493. It is the site of the very first documented confrontation between Europeans and the

Above and right: Salt River National Park, where Christopher Columbus landed on his second voyage to the region in 1493.

Kalinago (Carib Indians) that year. The area had been settled by the Igneri, a pre-Taino people, during which time it became an important cultural centre. A Tainan ceremonial ball court was unearthed here in 1923 and artefacts – including human sacrificial burials – from this site are on display in the National Museum in Copenhagen. In the 18th and 19th centuries Salt River Bay was used as an anchorage for ships loading produce from the many plantations around the island.

A bio-diverse coastal estuary, the Salt River Bay National Historical Park and Ecological Preserve encompasses the largest

remaining mangrove forest in the US Virgin Islands and provides a chance to glimpse endangered species such as the hawksbill turtle and the roseate tern. The area offers fantastic diving and i noted for its excellent examples of plate coral and huge sponges.

Follow the North Shore Road to **Cane Bay**, where the sea wall plunges to depths of up to 12,000 feet (3,600 metres). The upper level of the wall provides some world-class diving experiences. This pretty palm-fringed bay is also a popular snorkelling spot, as it is protecte by a coral reef and teems with myriad fish and corals.

urther along this stretch of
ɔastline, the luxurious Westin
ɑrambola Beach Resort and
ɑrambola Golf Club has a
hampionship Robert Trent Jones
ɔlf course that combines
ɔnderful vistas with challenging
ɔort. The resort is named after
ɪe star-shaped fruit which grows
ɪroughout the estate.

ɪe adventurous driver may wish
ɔ avoid the North Shore Road
ɪd take a trip through the
ountains and rainforest. You will
ɛed a four-wheel-drive vehicle
ɔr this trip, which will provide an
ɔ-close look at a sub-rainforest
ɪvironment, as well as offer
ɑgnificent views around St.
ɔix across to the other Virgin
ɪands on the horizon.

ɔllow the North Shore Road until
ɪe junction with Route 78
ɑrked "Scenic Road". It leads
ɔhill on a rough dirt road that
ɪickly narrows to a single lane,
ith fantastic views around each
ɛnd. When you reach Route 73
vhich is signposted), either turn
ght and head back down to the
ɔrth Shore Road, or go straight
ɪead on the road that slowly
ɪmbs up **Mount Stewart**. There
ɛ fabulous views down to the
ft of the Carambola Resort's
ɔlf course and the Caribbean on
ɪe right. It is worth stopping at

the summit to enjoy the distinctly
cooler temperature and savour the
stillness and fresh air. Further
along there is a choice to either
turn right and continue on Route
78 to **Ham's Bay**, or to turn left
onto Route 58 and drive through
to the west coast on the Creque
Dam Road. Route 78, the
favoured choice, leads along a
rocky road through a spectacular
landscape down to the dense 15-
acre (6-hectare) forest of the
Caledonia Valley. Teak, kapok,
cedar and mahogany trees tower
over the lush tropical flora below.
The road finally ends at Ham's Bay
and the US Coastguard lighthouse.
There is a gate on the right that
leads down an incredibly steep
path to the ruins of an old sugar
mill and eventually to
Black Rock Beach
and Wills Bay. These
stunning safe
beaches are well
worth the trip down –
and the scramble
back up!

Route 63 leads from
Ham's Bay down the
west coast to **Sprat
Hall Plantation** (Tel:
772-0305), a Great
House dating from
the days of the
French occupation of

St. Croix between 1650 to 1690.
This family home of Mrs. Joyce
Hurd is stacked with antiques
and offers several guest rooms
and other accommodation in
cottages scattered around the
grounds. It is idyllically situated
adjacent to a white sandy beach.
Equestrian tours are run from
here and anybody looking for a
full week of riding – ranging from
a gentle trot through the
rainforest, a canter along the
coast or a romantic moonlit ride –
will find this an ideal place to
stay. (See Where to Hang Your
Hat, page 143).

*Below: The Sprat Hall Plantation near
Frederiksted offers horseback riding
through the rainforest or along the east
coast beaches.*

Frederiksted

Frederiksted is comfortably toured in a day and is noted more for its Victorian than for its Danish architecture. The town was established in 1751 and is the second-largest town on the island. In 1867, the town was virtually destroyed by a huge tidal wave: 11 years later it was devastated by a fire started by the families of former slaves rioting in protest of their poor living conditions. The symmetric two-storey wooden frame houses on Queen Street are typical of the reconstruction that gives the town its character. The carefully laid-out streets are lined with shady trees, arcaded walkways and narrow alleys. There are also good examples of colonial architecture embellished with typically West Indian gingerbread fretwork and wrought-iron balconies. The **Visitor's Centre** is housed in the former 18th-century **Customs House** at the end of Custom Street. From here walk to **Fort Frederik**, which was started in the early 1750s and finally completed in 1776. It was named after the Danish King Frederik V

Left: Frederiksted features many examples of West Indian gingerbread fretwork. Above: Fort Frederik stands sentinel over the town's harbour.

and was built to protect the town's large sheltered harbour. Over the years the fort has undergone extensive restoration and today houses a museum and an art gallery. It was here in 184 that the declaration for the abolition of slavery was read by Governor General Peter Von Scholten. It was also the first for in the West Indies to unofficially recognise the United States on 25 October 1776.

Walk along the new pier for a scenic view of the town's old historic district and Strand Street. This waterfront shopping area is particularly noted for its distinctive arcaded buildings. At e corner of Prince and Market reets, **St. Patrick's Roman atholic Church** was completed in 843 and is interesting for its usual Gothic Revival-style nstruction of hand-cut stone ocks and Danish yellow brick. e interior features some fine amples of woodwork hand- afted by Frederiksted artisans, d the adjoining courtyard is filled th 18th-century gravestones. earby, **St. Paul's Episcopal urch** was built in 1812 and is a xture of Georgian and Gothic evival styles. The bell tower of posed sandstone was added in 848. The **Holy Trinity Luthern urch** is situated beside the old metery and dates from 1766.

ere are many interesting amples of 19th-century ctorian architecture, including **ctoria House** on the corner of rand and Market streets. This ivate home features elaborate rolls and gingerbread fretwork d has been fully restored lowing major damage wreaked Hurricane Hugo. The **Old othecary Hall** on the corner of ng Cross Street was built in 839 and was one of the only ildings to survive the fire in 878. It still houses a pharmacy d is a good example of the style architecture from this era.

The **Old Library** in Strand Street dates back to 1803. It is also known as Bell's House after its 19th-century owner, G.A. Bell, who fitted bells above the centre staircase. Along this section of Strand Street are some charming cafés and shops which overlook the waterfront.

Parts of Frederiksted are very run down and there are some large housing estates at the south end of town. It is therefore not advisable to wander around alone at night in the more deserted, badly lit areas – and particularly not wearing expensive jewellery or carrying large sums of cash.

St. Croix Safari Tours is based at Gallows Bay and is run by the knowledgeable and charming Sweeney Toussaint. Sweeney worked for many years as a hotel manager for one the island's premier resorts until Hurricane Hugo destroyed the property. He now runs a 25-passenger safari bus that takes visitors on informative tours around St. Croix. They regularly depart from Christiansted at 10am and take in the St. George Botanical Gardens, the Estate Whim Plantation and the Cruzan Rum

Below: Frederiksted is a major cruise ship port in the Caribbean.

flamingoes. Close by, the fabulous white sands of **Sandy Point** provide the perfect spot to witness the elusive "green flash" – an atmospheric phenomena that occurs as the sun sinks below the horizon. This beach is very isolated and it is inadvisable to go here alone or carrying valuables.

From Frederiksted it is worth taking Route 76, the Mahogany Road, which leads through densely-forested areas of towering mahogany, cedar and kapok trees to **St. Croix Leap** (Tel: 772-0421), a fascinating woodworking shop run by Cheech

Thomas. Here, Cheech and his team of fellow workers turn the trunks of dead mahogany trees into fabulous sculptured gifts ranging from inexpensive salad servers and bowls to individual free-form tables and chairs – eac a wonderful work of art. Local islanders are trained in the art o woodworking and the project is supported by the St. Croix Life and Environmental Arts Project.

Further along, the **Karl and Mari Lawaeetz Museum** (Tel: 772-1539) was a sugar plantation tha dates back to the mid-1700s. Th wooden-frame house that now

Distillery. Lunch is usually enjoyed on the waterfront at Frederiksted, followed by a tour of the rainforest and St. Croix Leap. Sweeney's tours are personalised and provide visitors with a unique view of Crucian life, as well as an overview on the history, politics, music, food and art of the island. (Tel: 773-6700; Fax: 773-3206).

To the south-west of Frederiksted, Sandy Point's refuge of **West End Salt Pond** is a bird-watcher's delight where some magnificent species can be seen, including

Above: Sandy Point Beach. Right: The Karl and Marie Lawaeetz Museum. Opposite: The magnificent bedroom in the Great House at the Estate Whim Plantation.

rves as the museum was built
1838. In 1896, Danish farmer
arl Lawaetz purchased the
state and used the ground to
ise cattle and grow vegetables.
e married his wife Marie in 1902
ad produced seven children, one
whom was a St. Croix senator
r 25 years until 1979. In 1996,
e St. Croix Landmarks Society
pened the house to the public as
museum; visitors are taken on
nducted tours around the
puse and grounds. The
xperience is fascinating and
ovides an authentic view of life
a a plantation in early 20th
ntury. It is open from Tuesday
Saturday from 10am to 4pm.

he **Cruzan Rum Distillery** is
cated off Route 64 in the south-
est of the island and is the
ome of the famous Cruzan Rum.
ur guides explain the
croduction of sugar-cane and
absequent growth of the sugar-
ne industry, the role rum has
ayed in Crucian history and the
irious processes involved in the
anufacture of rum. The tour
ads through the maturation
ieds and distillery, past the
pttling line to the tasting room.
slide show illustrating the
stilling process can be viewed
hile sampling the company's
irious rums.

The Estate Whim Plantation

Located off the Centre Line Road (Route 70) 2 miles (3.2 km) east of Frederiksted.

Telephone: 772-0598

Hours: Monday to Saturday from 10am to 4pm between 1 November and 30 April and Tuesday to Saturday from 10am to 3pm between 1 May and 31 October.

Entrance Fee: US$6.00 for adults and US$1.00 for children under 12.

Facilities: There is a wheelchair ramp into the Great House and the paths around the estate are accessible with some assistance.

This 18th-century sugar estate has been lovingly restored and gives an authentic feel of what life was like on St. Croix's sugar plantations in the 1800s. In accordance with the character of the plantation-era opulence, the interior is furnished with traditional West Indian furniture and antiques from Europe. The highlight of the tour is the European-style Great House, which was built in the 1700s in

Neo-Classical style and features thick walls of coral, sand and limestone. A dry moat surrounds the oval structure, which contains three rooms, an office gallery and a wing that was originally a separate kitchen. The Whim Museum's collection of exquisite furnishings includes a Danish piano, a mahogany four-poster bed, a rocking chair, a planter's chair – with extended arms designed to ease the removal of high boots – and a courting chair in the shape of an 'S'. The house is brimming with

that had been extracted from the cane was hand-ladled from copper to copper as the mixture boiled and thickened.

Many festivals and events organised by the St. Croix Landmarks Society, who have their headquarters here, are held in the grounds of the estate. These include Starving Artists' Day, candlelit chamber music concerts, the West Indian Antique Auction and annual house tours of private residences around the island.

The museum also maintains a genealogical library which is ope to the public. The helpful library staff will gladly assist visitors who may want to trace their ancestors who lived on St. Croix in years gone by.

The museum shop features a fascinating selection of native crafts, old prints and gift items. the adjacent furniture shop, the West Indies collection is a range of colonial furniture inspired by 18th- and 19th-century designs (*see Culture Club, page 99*).

charming antiques, such as brass chandeliers, inkwells and portraits of the original owners.

A guided tour leads through the grounds and includes a visit to a sugar-cane field, the village area – which originally consisted of 40 slave dwellings – and the sugar factory where a windmill still stands. The foundations are all that remain of the immense sugar factory where the juice

Above: The Estate Whim Plantation has been restored to provide an authentic look at life on a sugar plantion in the early 19th century. Right: A tour through the Estate Whim Plantation grounds leads to a restored windmill. Opposite: The St. George Village Botanical Gardens is home to an array of tropical flora and historic buildings.

St. George Botanical Gardens

Located left off Route 70 about 3 miles (5 km) from Frederiksted.

Telephone: 692-2874

Hours: 9am to 5pm daily between November and May and 9am to 4pm Tuesday to Saturday between June and October.

Entrance Fee: Minimal

Facilities: The garden is wheelchair accessible, except for the Tropical Rainforest and Arts of the Native Forest exhibits. All buildings open to the public are accessible to the disabled with some assistance.

The gardens are situated on 16 acres (4 hectares) of an 18th-century sugar plantation that was deeded to the St. Croix Garden Club in 1972. The area was also home to an Arawak village until about AD 900.

The plantation-era buldings have been renovated or stabilized to accommodate the public garden, and two worker's houses contain the gift shop, store rooms, restrooms, kitchen and offices. In 1972, the Great Hall was built to

join the two structures and serve as a visitors' pavilion. The garden is used to conserve native flora, and educational programmes on the horticulture, ecology and cultural history of the US Virgin Islands are conducted here.

The renovated plantation superintendent's house is now home to the garden curator, and also serves as the herbarium and research library. The renovated plantation buildings house blooming orchids, a visitor orientation centre and lecture room.

The stone ruins of other buildings were stablised and now act as backdrops and terraces for specialised plantings.

A self-guided walking tour leads through a semi-tropical rainforest environment, where a spectacular array of tropical flora abounds including philodendrons, ginger plants, lobster claws and orchids, all flourishing in a profusion of vivid colour. Meandering through the fascinating cactus garden, you will encounter giant kapok

trees and a garden which represents a miniature version of St. Croix's diverse ecosystem.

The medicinal herb garden is an educational display that includes plants commonly used in bush medicine and by herbalists on the US Virgin Islands today. Each plant is labelled and an informative leaflet explains its use and preparation.

eached!

f you conjure up a tropical paradise with endless white sandy beaches washed by arkling waters, bathed in nshine and cooled by gentle eezes, then the beach of your eams is waiting for you in the Virgin Islands. Whether your ea of heaven is to snorkel, uba dive, windsurf or simply ax in the sun, you will find a each to suit your every desire. e beaches offer everything om the calm, clear waters of e Caribbean to the wild, tamed seas of the Atlantic. hether you are looking for a cture-perfect isolated setting a long crescent of sand with tion-packed watersports, you ll not be disappointed – these ands are blessed with some of e most beautiful beaches in the orld. One point to remember is cess to beaches is a civil right the islands, but access to land at leads to them is not.

. Thomas

e 44 idyllic beaches on St. homas are one of the main asons for visiting the island. ey are all open to the public, t you invariably have to walk rough a resort to reach them. tel guests usually have access lounge chairs and floats that e off-limits to non-guests, so

you may feel more comfortable at one of the beaches – such as Magens or Coki – that are not linked to a resort. Some beaches on the north coast can only be reached by a four-wheel drive along rocky roads and over rough terrain. However, they are more secluded and definitely worth the effort. For complete solitude, why not hire a boat and discover your own private hideaway on one of the islets or cays offshore?

Driving west from Charlotte Amalie on Route 30 past the airport, the first beach you encounter is the lively **Brewer's Bay**, which is popular with students because of its proximity

to the university campus. Its west-facing aspect makes it a perfect place to watch the sunset.

Beyond Brewer's Bay there is a rough road which leads to the west end of the island and **Botany Bay**. It is a long drive with additional walking to reach there, but the snorkelling is great. Alternatively, leave Brewer's Bay and take the right fork for West End Road that runs to the northern coastline and **Hull Bay**. This tranquil and shady beach on the north shore faces **Inner and**

Left: At Buck Island on St. Croix, there is a fabulous underwater marine park with dazzling coral reefs. Below: Graceful palms silhouetted against a St. Croix sunrise.

Outer Brass Cays and is a favourite anchorage for fishermen and beachcombers. It is the best location on the island for serious surfing as it sometimes experiences some large Atlantic breakers. However, be careful not venture out too far unless you are a strong swimmer. There is a good bar and restaurant nearby for refreshments.

Travelling east from Hull Bay on the north coast, the stunning **Magens Bay** is situated at the end of tree-lined Route 35. The beach is among the top on many people's "best beach-in-the-world" list. A crescent of white sand edged by clear waters and fringed by lush greenery attracts the serious beach lover. The calm shallow waters are ideal for gentle swimming and the area is safe for small children. There is

an admission fee of US$1 per car, US$1 per person and 25c per child, and visitors can hire beach chairs, towels, snorkelling gear and most water-sports equipment. Picnic benches and barbecue grills are provided, making it a popular and often crowded place at weekends and public holidays. The beach bar serves tasty snacks and a nearby souvenir shop stocks a colourful array of beachwear.

Mandal Bay is a small beach on the north coast close to the Mahogany Run Golf Course. This is a quiet beach ideal for those looking to escape the crowds of the beaches further east.

Coki Beach on the north coast offers some of the best views on the island, with Thatch Key just across the Leeward passage. It is popular for snorkelling with both holidaymakers and cruise ship passengers because of its proximity to the fabulous Coral World underwater observatory (*see Sightseeing Spectacular page 40*). This beach buzzes with activity and local colour during the day. There is a lively beach bar and a stand selling cold drinks, meat patties and other snacks.

Water Bay is just a few minutes drive away and the setting for th Renaissance Grand Beach Resor The beach is a half-mile (1-km) arc of dazzling white sand where great watersports are available including jet skis, windsurfers, waverunners and sunfish sailboats. The on-site Chris Sawyer Dive Centre offers a number of courses which range from an introductory resort scub lesson right up to certified instructor level. Non-residents ar welcome in the various bars and restaurants in the resort.

Travelling down Route 38 towar Red Hook, you reach **Smith Bay Beach** (also known as Lindquist

...ach). It is easily reached along ...rough road between the ...yndham Sugar Bay Resort and ...vilions and Pools Hotel. The ...nds are lined with seagrape ...es and the area is peaceful ...d undeveloped.

...pphire Beach sits on the east ...ast and visitors can enjoy ...unning views of St. John and ...e British Virgin Islands from the ...lf-mile (1-km) stretch of soft ...hite sand. It fronts the Sapphire ...ach Resort, making the centre ...ittle crowded. However, by ...alking a little further towards ...ther end, you can usually find a ...ore secluded spot. Beach ...airs, snorkelling and wind-...rfing equipment are available ...r rent. The watersports centre ...n also arrange fishing or sailing ...ps. There is also a full service ...DI dive centre based here.

... the reef near Petyklip Point to ...e east, the snorkelling is ...xcellent, and this is a popular ...ot for windsurfing.

...ssup Bay is a gorgeous white ...ndy beach close to Cabrita ...int. Seagrape trees, cacti and ...ave plants provide a perfect

...ove left: The spectacular Magen's Bay ...ach on St. Thomas. Centre: The white ...nds of Solomon Beach on St. John. Right: ...nseekers enjoy the magnificent views ...und Hawksnest Bay on St. John.

tropical backdrop while you walk the beach, climb the rocks that are scattered over the sands, or wade in the rock pools. Watersports equipment can be hired from a concessionaire at the bus end of the beach. The headquarters of the US National Park Service is based here and they have a wealth of information about the islands, hikes and outdoor activities available.

Heading towards Charlotte Ama on Route 32, turn off on to Rout 317 to reach **Great Bay**, which is dominated by the palazzo-style Ritz Carlton. There are wonderfu views across to St. John and the sailboats wending their way between the islands.

Continue along Route 317 to rea **Secret Harbour**, a pretty beach with superb snorkelling, especial to the left near the rocky outcro Watersports, windsurfing lesson and equipment are available and would-be divers can sign up for a PADI scuba certification course.

Morningstar Beach is close to Charlotte Amalie. The pretty curve of the beach fronts the Morning Star section of Marriott Frenchman's Reef Hotel where

Left: The spectacular Sandy Point on St. Croix. Opposite: Lone fisherman casts his net into the clear Caribbean waters.

e watersports centre offers
rasailing, sunfish sailing,
ndsurfing, snorkelling and
uba diving. When visibility is
t obscured by the current,
orkelling is excellent near the
cks. **Limetree Beach** is next to
orningstar Beach and is set in
natural cove. This is a popular
ot for iguana watching.

. Croix

he largest island of the group,
. Croix offers many deserted
eaches fringed with pristine
ral reefs. There are acres of
touched land and spectacular
enery where visitors seeking
ace and tranquillity will find the
rfect place to relax. Columbus
each on the north shore is
lieved to be the site of the
olumbus 1493 landing on St.
oix. There are few facilities
re, but it is worth the trip just
stand on this historic site.

visit to **Buck Island** is a must on
ny trip to St. Croix. The sandy
each is beautiful, but the finest
easure is its underwater marine
ark and dazzling coral reef. The
and is part of the Virgin Islands
ational Park and was designated
National Monument because of
e barrier coral reef that lies off
eastern shores. It is home to
any bird species, including the

endangered brown pelican and
three species of turtle. The reef
includes fine examples of
staghorn, elkhorn and brain coral,
and the visibility is excellent. An
underwater trail has been marked
out for snorkellers where the
teeming marine life is colourful
and abundant. Visitors can reach
the island by one of the charter
companies and the trip takes
about one hour. Excursions are
either half- or full-day. (See
Sightseeing Spectacular, page 54).

At the north of St. Croix, **Cane
Bay** is a pretty palm-fringed cove
cut into the cliffs where the
waters can be quite choppy and
are sometimes large enough for

surfing. The sea wall which
plunges thousands of feet below
the surface offers excellent
snorkelling and scuba diving.

Follow the North Shore Road
towards Christiansted where a
number of hotels front some
attractive beaches around Little
Princess and Golden Rock. The
Cormorant Beach Club has a
particularly fine stretch of beach
where the snorkelling is good.
Continue on Route 75 and take
the 82 just out of Christiansted.
Beauregard Bay is the setting for
the **Buccaneer Hotel**. The facilities
within the hotel and great
snorkelling make this a lovely
place to visit.

Route 82 continues along the north east shore to **Tamarind Reef Beach**, a small, but attractive beach, with great views of Buck Island and Green Cay offshore. Green Cay is a National Wildlife Refuge and the island is home to many pelicans and herons. It is possible to take a charter out to the island for bird-watching trips. **Chenay Bay** is close by, with good watersports available.

At the east end of the island are the isolated sands of **Isaac Bay**. It is impossible to reach this point without a four-wheel-drive, but once there, you will find empty sands and calm waters. It can also be reached via a footpath from Jack's Bay.

The south coast has a number of pretty beaches including **Grapetree Beach**, which is a secluded spot with some occasional good waves. However, the more beautiful beaches are over on the west coast where **Sandy Point** offers miles of white sand in an isolated setting. There are no facilities and it is advisable not to leave any valuables unattended. Further up the east coast, north of Frederiksted, visit **Sprat Hall Beach**. Its many shells and other flotsam make this a spot a beachcomber's delight and the restaurant here serves great local fare. The nearby beach and Rainbow Beach Club has a lively bar, casual restaurant, watersports and volleyball.

St. John

St. John is THE place to get away from it all. Just a short ferry ride from St. Thomas, the island is blessed with some of the most lovely beaches in the Caribbean, particularly along the north shore which are all part of the Virgin Islands National Park. Some are more developed than others and thus crowded on weekends, holidays and in the high season. Take a trip along the south and eastern shores to find many secluded coves where your own private beach awaits!

Leaving Cruz Bay along the North Shore Road for about a half-mile (1 km), the first beaches are **Solomon** and **Honeymoon**. They are usually empty, which is probably due to the 15-minute hike required to reach them. Access is via a downhill path that leads from North Shore Road beside the sign for the Virgin Islands National Park Biosphere Reserve. There is a 10-minute walk down a trail which connects with the Lind Trail. Solomon Beach is off to the left and is the island's unofficial nudist beach. There are no facilities, but the powder-white sands and great snorkelling around the reef make the effort worthwhile. While swimming along the shallow reef between the two beaches, you are likely to be trailed by needlefish and houndfish.

Further along the north coast, **Caneel Bay** is actually a collective name for seven pretty beaches, six of which are so isolated that they can only be reached by boat unless you are staying at the Caneel Bay Resort. The seventh beach is open to the public and easy to reach from the main entrance of the resort.

ntinue along the north coast for
out a half-mile (1 km) to reach
wksnest Beach, which is lined
th seagrape trees. This is a
vely setting with good facilities
cluding rest rooms, cooking grills
d a covered shed for picnics. As
s the closest beach to Cruz Bay,
can often be crowded.

e beach has three distinct coral
efs that run out from the shore,
th sandy channels between.
ere, large shoals of damselfish,
rcupinefish, squid and peacock
ounder can easily be seen. On
e west side of the beach at the
cky point that is part of the
neel Bay Resort, there is a
scinating reef. Be careful
ough, as there are some tricky
rrents near the point and an
crease in boat traffic.

e road then leads past
openheimer Beach and
awksnest Overlook to tiny
mbie Beach. There is parking for
st three cars on the road and
e beach – which is down a flight
wooden steps – is usually
serted. The snorkelling is good,
t beware as the depths vary
nsiderably, leaving you
rilously close to sharp coral.
etween Trunk and Jumbie bays

posite: The fabulous Trunk Bay on St.
nn. Right: Local artist finds inspiration in
e colour, textures and light of Maho Bay.

there is a popular reef teeming
with schools of blue tang,
doctorfish and surgeonfish, as
well as the occasional nurse shark.

The fabulous sands of **Trunk Bay**
are just a few minutes further
along. This spectacular beach
takes its name from the
"trunkback" (leatherback) turtle
and, it is claimed has been voted
one of the world's most beautiful
beaches by *National Geographic
Magazine*. There is an excellent
650-foot (210-metre) underwater
trail that fledgling snorkellers can
follow with signs identifying the
marine life they may encounter.

This is a good spot to see rays and turtles, as well as parrotfish, tang and trunkfish. Snorkellers can also see stingrays cruising over the sandy shallow bottom. Trunk Bay is an occasional nesting site for turtles, which can be spotted swimming along the healthy coral formations east of Trunk Cay. In summer, the cay is surrounded with dark clouds of fry fish and patrols of large silvery-scaled tarpon darting amidst magnificent elkhorn, brain and fan coral.

While the fish may appear tame here, do not feed them as they will live a longer and healthier life by maintaining a normal diet. Cruise ships regularly come here for day trips and snorkelling, so check the schedules in advance if you are looking for seclusion. Crowded or not, this stunning beach is sure to please. It is an official National Park Service beach and an entry fee of US$4.00 per person is charged. Lifeguards are on duty and there are changing rooms, a snack bar, picnic tables, a gift shop, public telephones, lockers and snorkelling equipment rentals.

Left: Catamaran cruises provide an excellent way to tour the islands and visit some of the more inaccessible beaches and cays. Opposite: Cinnamon Bay Beach on St. John is a beautiful setting on the north coast.

rther up the hill **Cinnamon Bay** ·nts the National Park ·mpground. This is the longest, ·dest and often windiest beach · St. John and faces some ·etty cays just offshore. There · a small restaurant, rest rooms, · t shop and watersports centre · n by Rick and Cindy Metcalf. ·ey offer a complete range of ·atersports equipment, as well · windsurfing lessons (Tel: 693- ·02). One- and two-man kayaks · e available, as well as small ·ilboats. The windsurfing can be ·cellent, particularly in the ·ternoons. There is good ·orkelling off the point to the · ht where you will find angelfish · d large schools of purple · gger fish. Brightly-coloured · ral colonies have cemented · gether over the years on this · cient reef in a series of ·erhangs and ledges and ·vernous crevices. It is a long ·vim, but worth every stroke to · e the fabulous corals, sergeant · ajors, and grey and French · gelfish that inhabit the cay's ·aters. The currents can be · rong, so be cautious. A rocky · int north-east of the cay · rbours an incredible and ·verse collection of marine life, · t again, be conscious of the ·aves and currents in this area.

The Cinnamon Bay hiking trail and loop trail begins across the road from the beach parking lot (*see Sightseeing Spectacular page 46*).

Maho Bay is just off the road further along the North Shore Road. This popular beach is just below the award-winning Maho Bay eco-campground which is dedicated to the preservation of the environment. The campground offers informal talks on environmentally-friendly living which are open to non-guests. The beach is quiet and sheltered and a great place to spot turtles and schools of parrotfish. The

road then leads to **Francis Bay**, home to a wealth of birdlife, including the brown pelican and yellow-billed cuckoo. It is usually uncrowded and there is some good snorkelling around the reef at the far right end – but avoid the deep-water passage of Mary Point because of strong currents and boat traffic.

Waterlemon Beach is reached by driving past the Annaberg Plantation and parking where the single track road ends overlooking Leinster Bay. It is then a few minutes hike to a pretty beach where fantastic snorkelling can be

found off the small cay at the far end. The calm waters here are a great place to find turtles swimming amidst colourful sponges and large sea stars.

You will need a four-wheel-drive vehicle to reach **Lameshur Bay**, which is at the end of a long dirt road on the south-east coast. There are no facilities, but the snorkelling is wonderful and turtles are often seen. The ruins of the old plantation are a short walk down the road past the beach and there is a trail which leads over to Reef Bay. *(see Sightseeing Spectacular page 48).*

If you are looking for a great beach off the beaten track, the rocky beach of **Salt Pond Bay** on the scenic south-eastern coast,

next to Coral Bay and Drunk Ba is well worth exploring. It is a short hike down a hill from the park and the only facilities are a outhouse and a few picnic table scattered about. There are interesting tidal pools where yo can sometimes spot moray eels The snorkelling is good and you can be sure to see angelfish, snapper and occasional stingray particularly if you swim directly out from the shore heading for the rocks which break the surface. Take care not to leave anything valuable in your car, as reports of theft are common.

With over 200 miles (320 km) o beautiful coastline and year-rou near perfect weather, the US Virgin islands will guarantee the beach and holiday of your drear

Snorkelling

If there is magic here on earth, is surely found in the underwat world of the US Virgin Islands. F a total body and spirit experienc spending hours hovering weightless in the clear water wi leave you feeling refreshed and totally invigorated. With very litt experience anyone can don a mask, fins and snorkel and explore the many wonders hidd beneath the surface. Whether i an underwater wilderness you a

eking, or a self-guided
orkelling trail, the islands' are
essed with an incredible variety
marine habitats. As a general
e, always snorkel with a buddy
his is a great sport to share.

any of the snorkel sites can be
ached either by car or hiking
o them. For the more
venturous snorkeller, boat
ntals are available to transport
sitors to the outer cays and
ore remote areas. Check with
e experts at the local dive
ops for information on guided
orkel tours. These tours are
ry informative with underwater
perts identifying the diversity
marine life along the way.

e bays in The Virgin Islands
ational Park on the island of St.
hn are dedicated solely to
orkellers and other watersports
e restricted in these areas.
vim buoys are in place to mark
e "snorkel only" areas.

void the crowds in the high
ason by spending the early
orning hours snorkelling amidst
scinating marine creatures that
sappear from sight in the
idday sun. Several charter boats
d dive shops also offer night
orkel excursions. This is an
nforgettable experience and
fers a chance to catch a

glimpse of some of the unusual
creatures that only come out at
night. Lobster, eel and octopus are
night prowlers and the brightly-
coloured parrotfish surrounds
itself in a mucous-like cocoon to
avoid being preyed upon. If you
look closely at a piece of coral, you
will see the tiny holes where the
coral polyps live. The corals feed
at night and extend these polyps
to filter particles from the water.

Snorkellers are urged to take
responsibility at all times, so be
conscious of your fins and where
you are kicking or stepping. It is
easy to forget that coral is a living
organism and damage can be
done in an instant taking the reef
hundreds of years to repair.

Fire coral is a mustard-yellow
colour and grows on top of other
corals; it produces an unpleasant
buring sensation when touched.
Remember too: "If you don't
touch it, it won't touch you"!
Resist the urge to touch and
handle marine organisms as they
are more fragile or harmful than
they might look.

You can easily record your
experience with simple disposable
cameras or more advanced
systems, which can be rented at
the islands' dive shops. *Take only
pictures ... leave only bubbles.*

*Opposite: Junior beachcombers delight in
the treasures found in the sands on St.
John. Right: Snorkellers explore the reefs
around Mary Point on St. John.*

xtravaganza

n days of yore, pirates plied the blue waters surrounding these tropical islands. Sheltered bays d the sweet aroma of perfumed nd drew them to the islands' nerous natural harbours. rfectly quartered and protected well-watered anchorages, the ates would lie in wait for the avily-laden Spanish treasure ips that traversed the nearby aterways. Homeward bound, d loaded to the gunnels with ew World booty, they were easy ey on a massive scale. Today's ands, no less rich, no less uring, are set like sparkling wels in a sapphire sea, where istine beaches reflect the trade-mpered tropic sun. Above the aterline, the magnificent bays e blessed with a perfect mate. Below the surface, lies a rallel underwater universe – an credible array of colour and form at overwhelms the imagination.

adled by the Caribbean on one de and the Atlantic on the other, e US Virgin Islands sit just low the Tropic of Cancer and sk in year-round trade winds. ore than a million tourists a year sit, coming in by cruise ship, ane or sailboat in search of their rsonal Caribbean hideaway. But e islands, dubbed "America's radise", are also one of the

Caribbean's most popular diving destinations. Some of the world's most beautiful underwater landscapes are found in these waters where coral gardens teem with myriad tropical fish. Over a quarter of all visitors to the US Virgins spend part of their time snorkelling or scuba diving. Underwater options range from shallow patch reefs to some of the deepest wall diving anywhere in the world.

Each ocean has its own signature colour, taste and specialised life forms and here, the hues of the Caribbean bathe and highlight the warm colours of the marine life that make up the coral reefs. At night, under the penetrating radiance of lights and strobes, the corals explode into vivid reds and yellows – rich saturated colours that become embedded in the memory long after the warmth of the sun has faded.

As elsewhere in the Caribbean, water conditions in the winter can vary with the variations of pressure troughs. Water temperatures average 80°F (26°C) year-round and you can count on 60-100 feet (18-30 metres) of visibility at leeward dive sites unless heavy swells are

running, or plankton is blooming. For the rest of the year conditions are generally calm and clear and conditions are suitable for novices virtually everywhere. The major resorts or dive shops can arrange diving courses to suits all levels of ability.

These waters are home to many ledges, grottoes and swimthroughs dappled from their base to the waterline with a multi-coloured mantle of encrustation. For divers there is an incredible variety of underwater treasures waiting to be discovered. There are new and old wrecks, caves, tunnels,

Opposite: Hawksbill turtle swims through an underwater coral garden at Mingo Cay.
Below: French grunts dart through a coral overhang at Little St. James.

ledges and reefs. Pillsbury Sound is the passage between St. Thomas and St. John and is dotted with small islands, cays and pinnacles offering some fabulous dives – many less than a 30-minute boat trip from the shore. The sound is virtually enclosed and the water that moves in and out with the tides creates some exciting currents and excellent drift dives.

Near St. Thomas, the popular wrecks include the **Cartanser Senior**, the **General Rogers** – which was especially sunk to create an environment for the marine life to proliferate – and the **West Indies Trader** at Witshoal, a 400-foot (123-metre) freighter left standing upright on the sea bed at 40 feet (12 metres). These wrecks are covered in coral and are home to hundreds of species of tropical fish. The

alternative way to enjoy the underwater world of the islands is aboard the **Atlantis Submarine**, an electrically-powered submarine which holds 46 passengers and descends 150 feet (45 metres) on its one-hour tour. It departs from the cruise ship dock and also offers night dives.

St. Croix

St. Croix is known as an island of superlatives. It is the largest of the Virgin Islands with two distinct areas. It is less developed than St. Thomas, but larger and with more resorts and operators than St. John. St. Croix was formed by buckling of the earth's crust and is bordered by a sheer wall. Inshore patch reefs give way in places to vertical drops plunging to more than 600 feet (185 metres). The sea bed forms a thicket of mounding and branching corals while large tube and rope spongers hang from the wall face.

Dive operators enjoy a wealth of sites at the mouth of Salt River Canyon and there are also plenty of beach dives including one from the new pier at Frederiksted.

To the north-east is **Buck Island National Monument**. Half-day and full-day excursions take in a marked snorkelling trail, beach combing or a single tank dive. T[ ] is not the usual deep-water divin[ ] that St. Croix is famous for, but [ ] leisurely meander through shall[ ] sun-filled gardens of hard corals teaming with multi-coloured fish[ ]

There is an extraordinary 60- to 70-foot (18- to 21-metre) dive o[ ] an upside-down barge known as **Chez Barge** just outside the harbour. This location has becom[ ] a feeding station for large barracuda, green morays and others looking for a handout. On[ ] the experts should feed the fish[ ] but any competent diver can experience an exciting encounte[ ] with these huge creatures.

marine sanctuary has been
tablished to help preserve a
...al part of the ecosystem near
.lt River Canyon. (This is not
.ally a river as no fresh water
...ters the ocean here.) A deep
...ral canyon situated at the
...outh of a mangrove lagoon has
...ng been a favourite spot for
...vers of all levels of experience.
...any fish grow to maturity in the
...urky waters that surround the
...d roots of the mangrove trees
...efore venturing out to sea to join
...e coral reef community.

...vo of the best dives on St. Croix
...Salt River East and Salt River
...est – have been marked with
...uoys to help protect the corals
...om anchor damage. This area is
...ustained by the regenerative
...rce from inside the mangroves
...at hosts astounding marine life
...cluding the larger pelagics that
...uise the wall. Salt River East is
...pically dived from 45-130 feet
...4-40 metres), and Salt River
...est from 20-130 feet (6-41
...etres). At 100 feet (30 metres),
...ere are black coral trees and
...range sponges springing out
...om the east wall. The west wall
...as magnificent coral pillars
...wering out of the sand.

...urther west, it reaches closer to
...e shore permitting access to
...op-offs from land or sea.

Jimmy's Surprise is an advanced
dive from shore and an
intermediate level dive by boat.
A large cone shaped pinnacle
rises 90 feet (27 metres) and is
covered with warm coloured
corals, sponges and fascinating
invertebrate life. The ledge at its
base is a perfect spot to find
blackbar soldierfish. Spotted
morays fill the nooks and
crannies and shining blue chromis
are prolific.

Close to Salt River Canyon is
Shark's Shanty. Nurse sharks
ranging in size from 3-12 feet (1-
4 metres) favour this shallower
area, along with flying gurnards.

The most popular dive on St.
Croix takes place in the protected
waters of **Cane Bay**. From the
shore, a 15-minute surface swim
leads out to where the shallow
reef slowly reveals its dark
outline of coral and underwater
canyons. Garden eels are
frequently seen peeking out of
their holes in the sand. The long
swim is rewarded with a magical
descent into a land of incredible
sponges, circling schools of silver
sennet and clouds of blue tang.

*Opposite top: Cushion sea stars at Leinster
Bay on St. John. Centre: The pristene coral
reef at Life's Reef. Background: The US
Virgin Islands offer spectacular diving
amidst fabulous coral reefs and tropical fish.*

here are over 20 anchors embedded in the sand which date back hundreds of years to the era of piracy. At Cane Bay Dive Shop, divers can rent scuba equipment, take classes or go on an underwater tour.

Gentle Winds, **Rust-Op-Twist**, **Little Cozumel**, **North Star** and **Twin Palms** are but a few of the dives that the north shore has to offer, but watch the depths and current. The water is incredibly clear with a profusion of corals and reef fish.

The west end of St. Croix is most noted for great wreck diving and pier diving. Butler Bay has four different wrecks in progressively deeper depths. The most shallow is the **North Wind**, a tugboat 45 feet (14 metres) deep with many openings to swim through. A large barge sits in 50 feet (15 metres) of water, while beyond – 70 feet (21 metres) – sits another wreck, the **Suffolk Maid**. The deepest is the **Rosaomaira**, which sunk while off-loading cargo. The 200-foot (61-metre) freighter hulk rests furthest from shore. It sits at 100 feet (30 metres) and is marked with a mooring ball.

The new **Frederiksted Pier** is home to a profusion of sponges and corals as well as schools of snapper, goatfish and grunts. The old pier's famous sea-horses have moved to the new pier and are found in abundance around the deeper pilings.

St. Thomas

Divers in search of first-class diving will be spoilt for choice in St. Thomas. If you are here to dive, but your partner is not, you have found an island that will make you both happy. Divers can take their pick of the excellent reefs ablaze with tropical fish and massive rock formations projecting out of the sea, while land lubbers can entertain themselves with activities such as shopping, parasailing, boating and exploring the island.

Like an oasis in the sea, the **W.I.T. Shoal** brings life to the sandy stretch of ocean floor where it rests. This wreck puts St. Thomas firmly on the map for wreck diving. The maximum depth is around 90 foot (27 metres), but most of it can be explored in 60-70 feet (18-21 metres)

of water. The vessel is upright on the bottom and is over 300 feet (92 metres) in length. The wheelhouse towers reach to within 30 feet (9 metres) of the surface. While barracuda prowl the periphery, tight clusters of grunts swim in and out of the rigging. Five different decks can be explored and at the top of one ladder the safe sits, securely rusted shut.

Close to the *W.I.T. Shoal* and roughly 600 feet (184 metres) long lies the **Grain Wreck**. Sunk in 1960 and used as a training site for the US Navy, most of the ship is badly broken up, although the bow still defies ageing by rising 20 feet (7 metres) or more from

Opposite: Graceful Atlantic spadefish swim through a magnificent coral overhang. Below: Blackbar soldierfish.

the bottom at a sharp angle. It is not uncommon to spot a lone shark, turtle or schools of Atlantic spade fish here. Because of the ever-changing currents in this area, both wrecks are classed as advanced dives.

Buck Island and **Capella Island** sit side-by-side and can be viewed from the south shore of St. Thomas. Several bays with large boulder formations and reefs support a prolific marine life. The *Atlantis Submarine* bases its underwater operation between the two islands and fish-feeding stations have been successfully established. A sheltered cove on the west side of Buck Island is home to yet another wreck, the *Cartanser Senior*. Divers can

begin on the wreck, which is broken into several sections, venture across to a nearby reef and end up back on the wreck. Depths are 30-60 feet (9-18 metres). The site is protected a is shallow enough for snorkeller

Due south from Secret Harbour and resembling two humpback whales breaking the surface are **Cow** and **Calf Rocks**. The two rocks are over 300 feet (92 metres) apart and are usually dived separately at depths whic range between 10 and 45 feet (and 14 metres). Cow receives most of the attention due to its several impressive swimthrough blanketed with red and orange sponges – and its tunnels, archways and caves inhabited with vast schools of sergear majors and glassy sweepers Calf Rock is deeply incised in the shallow depths of 30-40 feet (9-12 metres) and horse eyed jacks, French grunts ar parrotfish are common.

The lee of **Little St. James Island** provides a safe haven away from the swells in the south. The shallows are flooded with light and teem with yellow wrasse and damselfish. Schools of goatfish forage through the white sand at the base of th

ef, which boasts stately stands
pillar coral. This is an excellent
oice for a night dive when the
ges are covered with lobster,
ffers, octopus and turtles.
pths range from 10-30 feet
9 metres).

e miles (8 km) south of Little
James in 20-90 feet (6-27
etres) of water, stands **French
p Cay**, which resembles a
ench beret rising several
reys out of the sea. Queen
gelfish, barracuda and Creole
asse frequent the area. Trips
e irregular because of the
rrents and weather conditions.

ki Beach, on the north-east
ores of St. Thomas, is popular
beach diving. There is
nstant movement of damsel-
h, parrotfish and sergeant
ajors. Here is Coral World, an
derwater observatory, and
arine Park beside the beach
ee *Sightseeing Spectacular page
.)* Night dives reveal tarpon
eding off baitfish lured in by the
vers' lights, octopus on the
ean floor and southern
ngrays sniffing for food. The
ach slopes off to 60 feet (18
etres) and currents can pick up
d run parallel to shore. Divers
e cautioned not to leave
luables in their vehicles while
ving here.

The wreck of the **Major General
Rogers** is nearby and is accessible
by boat. This old US Navy Coast
Guard buoy tender was scuttled
to create an artificial reef and it is
laden with orange cup corals.
Caesar grunts, goatfish and pairs
of French angelfish can be seen in
several locations around the
wreck. The 120-foot (40-metre)
vessel is upright in 60 feet (18
metres) of water.

The **Navy wrecks** are two barges
which were sunk off Limetree
Beach in 1946 and provide
excellent wide-angle photo
opportunities. The depths are
around 40 foot (12 metres) and
schools of angelfish, goatfish and
parrotfish can be seen here.

St. John

St. John, with its 51 bays and
small cays, is the smallest and
perhaps most beautiful of the US
Virgin Islands. The crystal-clear
aquamarine waters and abundant
marine life make snorkelling and
diving a favourite pastime here.

Pillsbury Sound separates St. John
from St. Thomas. It is 2 miles (3.2
km) across and is hemmed into
the north by a chain of cays. It is
these cays that help make up the
geographic boundary between the
Caribbean Sea to the south and
Atlantic Ocean to the north. Its

close
proximity to
St. Thomas
means that many of
the dive sites are shared
by operators from both
islands. One of the premier dive
sites close to St. John is **Carval
Rock**, just 10 minutes by boat
from Caneel Bay. This rock is
noted for its large numbers of
tarpon and clouds of silversides,
especially in late summer and early
autumn. Considered an advanced
dive because of its currents and a
seasonal north swell, depths vary
from 20-80 feet (6-24 metres).
There are many swimthroughs
encrusted with coral formations.

West of Carval Rock is **Congo Cay**.
Both sites are technically outside
of Pillsbury Sound and are linked
by an underwater ridge between
30 and 60 feet (10 and 20 metres)
deep. The better dives usually
occur on the west end of the cay,
where vast outcrops of coral lead
down to a sand shoot that spills
out in 80 feet (20 metres) of
water. There is an excellent drift
dive behind Congo Cay, with
depths that range from 35-80 feet
(9-18 metres). This is a great spot
to see the stingrays that frequent

*Opposite: Dazzling coral formations can be
found throughout the islands. Above:
Hawksbill turtle. Background: Shoals of
tarpon and silversides at Tarpon Rock.*

e area. The east end of the cay generally considered an vanced dive where overhanging cks eroded at the waterline ve created a sheer drop that is peted with orange cup and rgonian coral. Schools of bar ks and several species of romis can be seen. This spot is posed to weather so surface nditions can be choppy.

rther to the west and inside the otection of the Pillsbury Sound, e two cays separated from each her by a 30-foot (9-metre) gap. ngo and **Grass Cay** can be sily dived all-year round under y conditions. Both of the sites pport an extensive fringing reef the south. A favourite dive at ngo Cay is called the **Mounds of ngo**. The approach to the dive ds over a shallow well-lit rden of hard boulder corals, ge brain corals and some pillar rals. Parrotfish and schools of ue tang inhabit this site. The ef drops at a 45-degree angle ward a sandy bottom at 60 feet 8 metres) where dark patches isolated coral heads are mped together. Each mound pports its own dazzling array of opical fish, branching tube onges and delicate corals.

the calm protected waters off **ass Cay**, the 8- to 10-foot (2- to

3-metre) high purple sea fans and spreads of yellow finger corals crowd together competing for sunlight. The depths range from 20-60 feet (6-18 metres).

Thatch Cay is offshore to the west of Coki Beach. On the north side is **Bull Point** or **Boulder Bay**, a deep dive that drops to about 90 feet (27 metres) and teems with dazzling marine life. On the south, a shallow protected site known as **Veti Bay** ranges from 5-60 feet (2-18 metres), features a small wreck, hosts of iridescent vase sponges, slipper lobster and hordes of macro life. The legendary **Tunnels of Thatch** are in a nearby sheltered cove. Reserved for calm days, this is a shallow dive that leads through a series of long tunnels beneath an enormous rocky peninsula. Spotted drums, glassy sweepers and green moray inhabit the passageways.

Several unique sites include **Johnson's Reef** at 40-80 feet (12-24 metres) just in front of Trunk Bay, and **Steven's Cay**, near the entrance to Cruz Bay at 10-25 feet (3-8 metres), which is also an excellent night dive.

There is an extraordinary expanse of reef named **The Leaf** located beyond the white cliffs on the boundary of the waters of the National Park. It drops off on all sides to 80 feet (24 metres) and is still largely unexplored.

Divers can reach areas such as **Eagle Shoals** and **Flanagan Island** from Coral Bay. Eagle Shoals is marked on all charts as a hazard to navigation, but to divers this area is an utter delight. This relatively shallow dive at 20-50 feet (6-18 metres) is most noted for a large doughnut-shaped grotto with at least six openings. Nurse sharks, an occasional reef shark and octopus are often seen.

Opposite and below: The reefs in the US Virgin Islands are a fantasy world filled with a kaleidoscopic variety of colour, shape and form. It is here that the rich diversity of nature is displayed with spectacular effect.

flor

nd fauna

When the Lesser Antilles were forced up to the earth's surface from the ocean floor during a series of fiery volcanic explosions more than 150 million years ago, exotic landscapes were created on which a tapestry of tropical flora has evolved. Many of the vivid floral species found in the Virgin Islands are those which have come from other lands. In the years which followed the voyages of great explorers like Christopher Columbus, an exchange of cultures began, the influx of vegetation – either for food or aesthetic purposes – but both equally valued.

In relatively more recent years, the progress of mankind has had an enormous effect on the environment which has resulted in the extinction of many species of indigenous flora and fauna. Fortunately conservationists have realised the impact of modern commercial development on the eco-systems. Strenuous efforts continue to be made to safeguard the natural surroundings by establishing

Photographs clockwise from top left: delicate bloom; fabulous night blooming cactus; gardens around the US Virgin Islands abound with a profusion of colour; tiny banaquit sipping nectar from a century plant; dazzling red hibiscus – a symbol of the tropics. Right: Glorious double hibiscus.

national parks and protected areas. Most of St. John, as well as Hassel Island in St. Thomas harbour, is preserved as part of the Virgin Islands National Park. The headquarters of the National Parks Service is at Red Hook on St. Thomas; along with the Island Resources Foundation (Tel: 775-6225), it is open to anybody studying wildlife, tourism and the environment.

St. Croix is home to the most recently-designated national park in the United States, the 912-acre (365-hectare) Salt River Bay National Historical Park and Ecological Preserve. This historic site, where Columbus landed on 14 November 1493, will protect an area rich in evidence of continuous occupation dating from AD 300, as well as a diverse array of ecological treasures.

Over time, the gentle tropical climate of the Caribbean has provided the perfect environment for a spectacular variety of plant and animal life. Diverse

vegetation and limitless varieties of nature abound on these dots in the Caribbean Sea where an entire spectrum of natural habitats exist. The lush tropical vegetation teems with exotic fruit trees, myriad floral species that bloom all year round and the massive trees of the ancient rainforest that blankets half of St. Croix. The rugged Atlantic coastline demonstrates the harsh conditions survived by only hardy xerophytic vegetation, yet is bordered by the life-sustaining mangroves. These protect the shores from wave erosion and provide a safe haven for a host of marine life and bird species – including the heron, egret and humming-bird. The black mangrove is a favourite habitat for the honey bee.

St. Thomas has over 1,220 different plant species on its 32 square miles (83 square kilometres). St. Croix is the most exotic island with 42 different species of orchid growing virtually anywhere, and twice that number in morning glories.

Flower Garden

Columbus recorded that St. Croix was a lush tropical garden when he first landed there in 1493. With the subsequent arrival of the European settlers, the land was cleared for the cultivation of sugar and cotton and the forests became a rich source for timber, fruits and spices. Vast areas of precious forest land were decimated to provide timber for the construction of homes and warehouses, as well as for burning as charcoal. The islands' plants and trees have played a vital part in its evolution as they have provided a basis for the economy, a sanctuary for wildlife and the foundation for many local herbal remedies.

The most common flower of the Caribbean is the **hibiscus**, with over 200 known species and a grand array of colours. The trumpet-shaped flowers have four to five petals creating the base for the characteristically long stamen tube. The double varieties have a dual set of petals and resemble a rose from a distance. The most distinguished

and delicate species is the coral hibiscus. The lacy petals curl upward while the protruding stamen tube hangs down sever inches below.

Originally brought to the region from Hawaii, many varieties car be found everywhere – from the manicured gardens of the grand hotels to the cultured botanical displays found at St. George Botanical Gardens on St. Croix. Situated in 16 acres (6 hectares of the prehistoric rainforest area visitors here will find more than 1,000 species of flowering plant and trees.

oviding borders and hedges for most every property on the lands is the dazzling profusion f colour provided by the **bugainvillea**. This climbing, horny shrub comes in a grand ssortment of colours, including urple, magenta, orange, pink, se, white and mixed ombinations. The plant was riginally brought to the region om Brazil in the 18th century.

he national flower is the yellow **nger thomas**, whose delicate umpet-shaped flowers bloom hroughout the year, while winter ees the reign of the brilliant red white **poinsettia**, which riginated in Mexico.

here are over 500 species of **chid**. These delicate plants are ell suited to this tropical nvironment and grow profusely ith little supervision. The orchid mily is the largest plant type in he world, with over 30,000 hown varieties.

he heavily-scented flowers of he island are harvested for their agrance. **Jasmine**, **white ginger** nd **gardenia** are blended by

hand with leaves from the **bay berry tree** and the essence of citrus fruits to produce popular Virgin island perfumes.

The cultivation of **sugar cane** dates back nearly 12,000 years and has probably shaped the economy of the Caribbean more than any other plant. The sugar plantations were central to the lives of slaves in the production of molasses, rum and the slave-trade itself. The sugar cane plantations of St. Croix, which date back to the 18th century, are one of the most interesting features of the island. Although

sugar-cane is no longer grown commercially, it can still be seen growing in the wild. After the canes – which grow up to 12 feet (4 metres) in height – were cut, they were crushed to extract the juice. This process was followed by boiling the juice until the sugar crystallised, leaving molasses, which is used to make rum.

The original planters described the fertile volcanic soil as "gold" because every inch of St. Croix is extremely fertile and many of the islands' estates had their own mills, the remains of which can still be seen today.

r left: multi-coloured wildflowers carpet e hillsides of St. John during the rainy ason. Centre: Christopher Columbus corded that St. Croix was a lush tropical rden when he first landed there. Right: agrant pink frangipani.

here are many species of **palm** nd other common tree species cluding **kapok**, **yellow cedar**, nnamon, **maho** and **sandbox**. any exotic fruit trees grow here cluding **mango**, **pineapple**, eadfruit, **soursop** and **guava**. he **sea grape** flourishes on ndy coastal areas and has athery, red-veined ovate leaves. s purple fruit, with its white pulp nd slightly bitter taste, is used make jelly and drinks.

he essential feature of life on e island is the **coconut palm**, ery part of which is put to a od use. The leaves are used as atch for roofing, hats or askets and the coir is used to ake rope, brooms and brushes. he oil is used in the manufacture soap and shampoo. Visitors ill regularly encounter machete-ielding locals chopping the tops f green coconuts and it is efinitely worth stopping to enjoy e milk contained in the seed, hich makes a refreshing drink.

espite their grace and the shade ovided, it is wise to avoid cting beneath palm trees to oid the danger of being hit by a

p left: The spectacular century plant only wers once during its 20-year lifespan. ttom left: A variety of cactus is found roughout the islands. Right: Palms urish on the hillsides around St. Thomas.

falling coconut. The trees are extremely hardy and can survive for long periods without rain. They grow in sand and reach heights of up to 80 feet (24 metres). Their fruit are among the largest seeds in the world, and each tree can produce up to 100 per year. The seed, with its layer of coconut, is surrounded by a hard outer shell, which in turn is surrounded by a layer of copra and finally a green husk. The coconut palm originated in the Pacific and Indian oceans, and the seeds literally floated across the seas.

The **breadfruit tree** was introduced to the West Indies by Captain Bligh of *Bounty* fame in 1793. It was his attempt four years earlier to import young breadfruit trees from Tahiti that led to the infamous mutiny. Bligh's orders were to take the trees to the region to provide a cheap food supply for the slaves. His regime was tyrannical, and he ordered that his precious cargo be carried onto deck each morning and back down into the hold at night. It is claimed that when he ordered that the saplings be watered with the meagre supply of water intended

for the crew, the mutiny was sparked. Nonetheless, the breadfruit tree was successfully introduced to the Caribbean. The large green fruits are eaten either fried, baked, roasted or cooked up into a hearty rich soup.

The **manchineel tree**, which is found on many beaches, is highly poisonous. This medium-sized tree with green and glossy ovate leaves produces a sap that causes skin blistering. Its fruits, which resemble crab-apples, are extremely toxic and the milky sap from the tree causes blisters and has been used as a poison. Do not touch or eat the apples and do not sit under the tree during a shower, as the rain will wash the sap onto your skin. The sap is so poisonous that the early Caribs used to dip their arrowheads into it before going into battle.

**WARNING!
MANCHINEEL TREE**

THE LEAVES, BARK, AND FRUITS OF THESE TREES CONTAIN A CAUSTIC SAP WHICH MAY BE INJURIOUS IF TOUCHED. COLUMBUS DESCRIBED THE SMALL GREEN FRUITS AS 'DEATH APPLES'. THE TREES ARE COMMON ALONG CARIBBEAN SHORES. AVOID CONTACT WITH ANY PART OF THIS TREE!

The **dwarf gommier** gives off a fragrant resin and is locally referred to as the "turpentine tree". The Carib Indians used th sap to treat internal bruises an sprains. The bark of the tree which is shiny with a reddish tir is constantly peeling. Locals often refer to it as the "tourist tree", because of its similarity t tourists who spend the first da of their vacation peeling from sunburn! This tree played a role in the island's heritage as it wa used by the Amerindians to fashion their canoes.

The **gumbo limbo** contains a medicinal sap which smells like turpentine and is used in the manufacture of ink and varnish

The island has three varieties o the towering cedar tree, white being most common. The **Spanish cedar** is highly valued f its fragrance and the **white ced** is popular in the manufacture o furniture as well as for its medicinal uses. The **Honduras mahogany** grows throughout th tropics and is extremely valuab for its dense timber. A popular ornamental tree is the **fiddlelea**

Left: Sea grape trees grown in abundanc on the shores of St. Thomas. Centre: The papaya is one of the many tropical fruit trees which grows throughout the islands Right: The dazzling flamboyant tree.

Originating in Central America, the **frangipani** or pagoda tree forms a broad canopy of branches from which the fragrant five petal blossoms emerge. This spectacular flowering trees thrives well in drier areas and will drop its leaves to conserve the moisture needed for its flowers.

, so called because of its violin-aped leaves. The yellow wering **Brazilian rose** is used as tural fencing and its bark is ed for making rope. The **coral ad tree** from Asia produces a avy wood which is used in the nstruction industry and its ight red seeds, known as umble beads", are used by vellery makers. Imported from adagascar, the spectacular mboyant, with its crimson ooms tinged with orange and llow, can be found throughout e islands. According to folklore e flamboyant is a symbol of erlasting love. The **African tulip** ee produces circular clusters of diant orange-red flowers rrounding large brown seed ds. This tree is so brilliant when bloom it is often referred to as he flame of the forest".

In typically Caribbean style, the locals give charming names to plants such as the "**cutlass tree**" with its scabbard-shaped blooms, "**the sensitive plant**" that curls when touched, "**man's heart**" that changes colour daily, "**mother in law's tongue**" whose dry pods rattle, the parasitic "**love vine**" that smothers its host, the fast-growing "**quick stick**" and the thorn spiked "**monkey-don't-climb**" or "**sandbox**" tree. The latter gets its name from the colonists' use of its wood to fashion small boxes to hold blotting sand in the era of the quill pen. The **century plant**, so called because it only flowers once during its 20- to 25-year lifespan, has stems that grow quickly; these are cut back and decorated by locals as recyclable Christmas trees.

There are many species of grass on the islands which prevent soil erosion and provide a natural habitat for many creatures. **Guinea grass** grows profusely and can cut the skin easily, while others, such as **Bermuda grass**, are cultivated into verdant lawns even when water is in short supply. Grassy Point, on the south side of St. Croix, is one of the few shores without a sandy beach and here the blades of grass are washed by the ocean waves. The arid easternmost point of St. Croix, at Point Udall, is where cacti and other succulents thrive in the warm dry climate.

Birdlife

Although man has hunted many bird species to extinction, the song of the morning dove or mountain pigeon can still be heard in the wooded hillsides of the Virgin Islands. These specks of land in the Caribbean act as staging posts for migrating birds to and from the Americas and as a result the region is a Mecca for ornithologists. Migratory visitors include the **bobolink**, **yellow-bellied sapsucker**, the **Caribbean martin** and the **Jamaican vireo**. There are such dainty birds as the **green-throated hummingbird**, which hovers above flowers, sipping the nectar, and there are the hooligans of the bird world such as the **peregrine falcon**, which drops like a bomb from the skies in search of its prey. The power-diving **brown pelican** is a magnificent fisher with its two-gallon (7-litre) pouch and competes for its catch with the **laughing gull**, famous for its distinctive cry. The locals say that this scavenging bird will even sit on the head of pelican to snatch any fish hanging from its huge beak. The colourful wild parrots that had the good fortune to escape the ubiquitous mongoose live in remote areas, and wild parakeets provide flashes of green and yellow in the tree tops at the break of day. The national bird of the US Virgin Islands is the **yellow breast** (or **bananaquit**), and its tastes for fruit and nectar explains why it is also known as the sugar bird. The magnificent **frigate bird**, **great blue heron** and **white-tailed tropic bird** can also be spotted around the coast.

Lurking Lizards

Six species of lizard are native to the islands and are often seen scuttling though the bush in search of their prey. They are very adaptable, being aquatic, arboreal, terrestrial and able to survive harsh desert-like conditions. A once endangered species of ground lizard has been discovered on St. Croix's Green Cay. The vast majority of reptiles found on the island are harmless to man, although there are many groundless superstitions that surround the small geckos, snakes and iguanas that live here. The common green-coloured **tree lizard** is distantly related to the iguana, and the males demonstrate dramatic mating rituals when they expand their throats, bob their heads and hiss at their intended.

The **iguana**, which can grow up to 6 feet (2 metres) in length – including its long, whip-like tail – is mostly green, but does have some brown cells that can expand to provide a better camouflage. They can still be found in the wild in trees or low scrub, but their numbers have declined since the days when the iguana was an essential part of the Amerindian diet. Today these reptiles are protected, although islanders still consider them a delicacy.

Iguanas can be found asleep in the trees at Limetree Beach where, if you can spot these reclusive and

them from extinction they are being bred in captivity and reintroduced to Congo Bay. They feed on small animals and secure their prey by wrapping around the victim's body and constricting their intake of air. They are not large enough and definitely not aggressive enough to attack humans.

Whale-watching takes place from February to April; the US Virgin Islands lie in the migratory passage of the humpback whales. Local tour operators can help in arranging boat trips to watch these magnificent creatures on the annual journey.

The islands' only surviving indigenous mammals are the **Jamaican fruit bat**, the **cave fruit bat** and the **red fruit bat**, which play a crucial part in the survival of the forest eco systems by scattering seeds and pollens.

The **mongoose** was introduced to the region

from India during the plantation days of the early 1800s to help control the population of rats that attacked the sugar cane. However, rats are nocturnal and mongoose are not, so they only succeeded in decimating most of the parrot and snake population, along with vast tracts of native flora. Although measures have been taken to protect the birds and their habitats, the mongoose population of the US Virgin Islands is among the highest in the world. Despite their less than rosy reputation, these furry animals have endeared themselves to children and entered folklore as the unofficial mascot of St. John.

A note of warning for drivers: beware of chickens, pigs, goats and cows, because on all three islands these creatures all have the right of way on the roads!

avily camouflaged creatures, u can try to feed them. After eir precarious mating process h up in the trees, the female oks for the best patch of land lay her leathery eggs by gging numerous holes in the und. They are herbivorous and eir favourite food is the biscus flower.

uring a tropical downpour listen t for the **coki frog** and the merous species of **toad** that company the noise of the nfall with a deafening chorus croaks. Between showers ey successfully keep the ands' insects at bay, which can herwise be a tremendous isance, particularly mosquitoes d wasps.

ere are no poisonous snakes the Virgin Islands, but look out r the **tree boa** which likes to de in coconut palms. To save

Left: Dainty hummingbird. Bottom left: The endangered brown pelican. Above: Coki tree frog. Right: Green-faced iguana.

lub

As much a part of the island experience as the golden sands and the azure seas, the arts are an integral part of any visit to the US Virgin Islands. The thriving cultural scene is strongly inspired by everyday island life, and the visual arts are thus imbued with a vibrancy and passion seldom found elsewhere. The strong mix of cultures reflect the island's past and there is a strong tradition of arts and crafts. Indeed, the art world flourishes, with numerous galleries exhibiting the varied works of talented local and international artists.

Paintings in oils, acrylics or watercolours infused with the colour and light of the Caribbean are tremendously popular with visitors The artistic talent to be found on the islands is complimented by the wide range of readily-available natural resources. A wealth of local talent produces beautiful craftwork, including pottery, wood carving, basket weaving, shell art,

Top left: Colourful pastel work by Janet Cook Rutnik. Top right: Okidanokh Handcraft have a beautiful shop in Royal Dane Mall in Charlotte Amalie. The walls are decorated with hand-painted storybook illustrations and the jewellery is one of the best buys on the island. Left: The islands' dance traditions are a strong reflection of African heritage. Right: Pastel work by Janet Cook Rutnik.

sculpture and needlework. Most artists are happy to talk about their work and many will allow visitors to watch them create their magnificent pieces, which adds another dimension to one's appreciation of the process.

The Virgin Islands are home to an abundance of cultural artists, most noticeably Austin Peterson, whose "painters' posse" decorate the islands' roadways with colourful murals. Other artisans and sculptors who draw their inspiration from their surroundings, exhibit their works in more conventional galleries. The **Virgin Islands Council of the Arts** was established in 1965 and Arts Councils today exist on all three islands to sponsor cultural events and promote arts and crafts. There are regular shows hosted at different venues and many restaurants decorate their walls with the work of local artists. Sponsored by the Chamber of Commerce, the Hospitality Lounge in the Grand Hotel on St. Thomas showcases works by local artists each month, and Fort

Christian Museum also hosts events every two months. All the paintings are for sale.

Those in search of unique perspectives on island life should visit the **Tillett Gardens** on St. Thomas, home to artists working in silk-screen, shells, coral, stained glass, wax, copper, painted enamel and clay, as well as more traditional mediums.

"I got involved in art when I was around six or seven years old," says Sonny Thomas, master printer at the **Jim Tillett Printing Studio** in the Tillett Gardens. "I hated it and did it just to stay out of trouble. Over the years my

Below: Spectacular mosaic by Lisa Crumrine. Her work is on display at Syzergy Gallery at Coral Bay, St. John.

love for the art, along with my talent, grew; now I come here five, sometimes six days a week, perfecting my craft."

In the cool shade of the gardens, Sonny prepares his canvas, smoothing the edges of the white cloth along his easel. He carefully chooses his wooden frames with delicate pieces of silk stretched across them. Each piece of silk is imprinted with an intricate design which he will use to create his masterpiece. He works quickly and smoothly, applying layer after layer of colour using a proficiency and skill born of his experience.

Sonny is just one example of the hundreds of artists – painters, sculptors, craftsmen, musicians, dancers, writers and storytellers – who help to make St. Thomas a culturally enriching place to visit. These creative individuals find their calling in a number of ways, whether it be through formal education, like the notable local artist Peter Gonzalez, a participant in the Public Arts Programme, whose lithographs of island life are sold in galleries and

Top: The Bajo el Sol Gallery at Mongoose Junction on St. John displays a fabulous collection of fine art. Centre: Skinny Legs at Coral Bay on St. John is home to some faulous artists studios. Bottom: The work of Aimee Trayser is displayed at Mongoose Junction in Cruz Bay.

gift shops; through apprentice- ship, like Sonny Thomas, who studied under Jim Tillett, a worl renowned silk-screen artist; or through self-exploration and meditation, like Abel Fabri, who creations in gold and gemstone at **Okidanokh Goldcraft** in Tillett Gardens delight and impress. "I is a continuous process," says Fabri as he shows some of his fabulous designs of exquisitely detailed silver and gold jeweller "You try to put something of yourself in the medium you wor with and hope that it will appea to, and affect, other people." Okidanokh also have a beautiful shop at the back of the Royal Dane Mall in Charlotte Amalie where the walls are decorated with pastel coloured, hand- painted storybook illustrations.

Also based at Tillett Gardens is Albert Thomas, who hand- screens maps and serigraph scenes on canvas at the **Tillett Art Gallery**. He greets visitors a the studio and explains the silk- screen process as he works at his 40-foot (13-metre) long tabl The gallery also sells oils, water colours, acrylics and a variety o prints by several local artists.

Refreshments are close at hand **Polli's** garden restaurant and ba set beside a tiny fountain

flair for utilising many of the bounties that nature has provided. Some local artisans on St. John and St. Croix still weave baskets from hoopvine and wist vines. In the French community on St. Thomas, it is possible to find someone who will plait a made-to-order bonnet or demonstrate the technique of making fish-pots from tied sticks. Local craft shows sell many and varied pieces of crochet and embroidery.

At the **Native Arts and Crafts Co-operative**, next door to the Visitor's Bureau in Charlotte Amalie, everything on sale is island-made – ceramics, place mats, island dolls, baby blankets, straw hats, tropical wall hangings, local honey and guava preserves. More than 40 local artists – including school children, senior citizens, and people with disabilities – create an ever-changing array of hand-crafted items, which also include African-style jewellery, quilts, calabash bowls, carved-wood figurines, woven baskets, straw brooms, note cards and cookbooks.

Visitors who appreciate the rich dark tones of mahogany will be overwhelmed by the collection at the **Whim Plantation**, where St. Croix's master craftsmen have recycled mahogany trees felled by

hurricanes into hand-carved works of arts and furniture. They also sell unique beautifully made items of furniture including armoires, sofas, chairs, hurricane lamps and tables based on traditional West Indian designs. The furniture is manufactured by Baker Furniture in North Carolina and is 35 per cent cheaper than the mainland price inclusive of insurance, packing and shipping to the United States.

Left: Delicate metal sculpture outside Best of Both Worlds Gallery on St. John. Below: The talented Lisa Crumrine creates spectacular mosaics in coloured glass.

ovides a cool setting for lunch, nner and drinks through the day.

he work of some of the US Virgin ands' most popular artists, articularly those who depict and scenes and people, is splayed in originals, prints and cards. Galleries represent a umber of painters from islands in e West Indies and there are ten exhibitions by artists, some ell known on the island, others ternationally recognised.

om the *pistarckle* broom made sticks and bush to home-made arcoal that fuel slow-cooking ts, the Virgin Islanders have a

Jonna White, who opened her first gallery on St. Thomas in 1978, now has a bright and spacious gallery on the waterfront near Palm Passage. She has developed a highly personalised style, working with etchings on hand-made papers in the dazzling colours synonymous with the Caribbean. Many of the etchings are large and they can be bought framed or unframed with shipping to the mainland at no extra charge.

Tropical Memories, near the waterfront end of Royal Dane Mall in Charlotte Amalie, is full of island art and craft items. It is presided over by a colourful owner known as the Captain – creator of the unique footstools available in the store.

Situated close to Coral World, the **Kilnworks Pottery and Art Gallery** is the creation of artist Peggy Seiwert who produces and sells an incredible selection of pottery, including a popular line of lizards in raised relief. Peggy also sells paintings, jewellery, sculpture and glass made by other local artists. Look out for the large green iguana holding the sign on the main road.

Original paintings in bright tropical colours, hand-worked textiles and

intricate local crafts fill the walls and brim from the shelves at th **Colour of Joy**, a gallery and gift store in Red Hook's American Yacht Harbour. Pretty lightweigh dresses, sarongs and sandals ar also stocked.

Calypso in the A.H. Riise Mall or St. Thomas sells a wide selectio of charming souvenirs, including sauces and jellies, hand-made local jewellery, spices and herbs island music and Caribbean cookbooks.

The owners of **Folk Art Traders** on St. Croix, Patty and Charles Eitzen, regularly travel to Guyan as well as Haiti, Jamaica and elsewhere in the Caribbean to find treasures for their shop. Th baskets, ceramic masks, potter jewellery and sculptures are a unique blend of folk art tradition

Bajo El Sol in Mongoose Junctio on St. John is a stunning airy gallery owned by Kat Sowa, Aimee Trayser and Les Anderso (Tel: 693-7070). The talented an beautiful Kat has been living an painting in the Caribbean for 12 years and her style is a reflectio of the tropical palette and sun-drenched colours that are part c everyday life on the islands. She trained as an architect as well a: an artist and the achievements

information). Aimee Trayser started work as an artist in the late 1960s and her work has been heavily influenced by her travels to Mexico and Hawaii. She works in many different media and creates surreal dream-like images on mystical collages which largely feature the blues and greens of her tropical surroundings. Les Anderson uses traditional methods and his work echo the rich traditions of the islands' African and European heritage. He works in watercolours, oils and produces hand-pulled heliogravure prints.

Aase Pedersen of **Wicker Wood and Shells** on St. John has developed an outstanding gallery for island art. Look for the stone staircase leading to the floor above her shop. Here she has gathered paintings, sculptures,

s inspirational woman are emingly limitless. Her work is rt of collections around the orld and she has been cognised throughout her career r her contribution to the arts. t captures moments in time in r fabulous land- and seascapes d delights in portraying the nple pleasures of life. Her aim is "stir people's understanding at the essence of all humanity are in the same needs however ncealed". Kat has also designed d hand-built probably the most mantic place to stay on St. John. rie is the result of a six-year our of love and is perched on e of the highest peaks on the and. (See *Where to Hang Your t, page 137* for further

carvings and pottery from local and regional artists. Her talent for selecting some of the best representations of island paintings makes the gallery's one-person shows a resounding success.

At Skinny Legs in Coral Bay in St. John, the **Syzergy Gallery** displays beautiful creations in silver and stone by Serena van Rensselaer and pastels and watercolours by Tracy Eaton. Spectacular glass mosaics by Lisa Crumrine are also available here and one can often find her hard at work outside the gallery. Lisa is happy to demonstrate her craft and talk with visitors about the inspiration behind her work.

Opposite: Magnificent mixed media work of art by Janet Cook Rutnik. Centre: Kat Sowa creates a watercolour masterpiece of Trunk Bay on St. John. Below: Colourful votifs available from Syzergy Gallery on St. John.

Cruzan Gold in Christiansted Harbour on St. Croix is owned and run by former commercial diver Brian Bishop. His studio is a shady terrace and visitors are invited to sit and watch him at work. In addition to his own, originally-design of the Cruzan bracelet, he produces a variety of gold and silver jewellery.

St. John's internationally exhibited artist, **Janet Cook-Rutnik**, has lived in the US Virgin Islands for 30 years. Renowned Washington art critic Ferdinand Plotzer has likened her work to "colourful, mellifluous blends of abstract art and figurative elements… to quiet-tone poems inspired by personal loss and the search for spiritual fulfillment."

Janet's work presents a fascinating and exotic sense of the ethos and ambience of the Virgin Islands and she has established herself as one of the most original artists in the region. Her thought-provoking paintings and mixed media pieces reveal an artistic genius who, with passion and style, has been able to translate in her work the elements that define the colour and light of these islands.

Janet welcomes visitors to her studio at Guavaberry Farms on St. John where she is happy to show her many beautiful works on display and talk about the inspiration behind her talent.

Charles Hawes is an internationally-recognised artist who was born in West Virginia in 1909. He has lived in the US Virgin Islands for over 30 years and his first water-colour exhibition in 1964 heralded a tradition that spanned the next three decades. All his paintings capture the vitality of life in the West Indies and demonstrate a deep affection for the islands ar their people.

Tradition and Belief

Forming a diverse human tapestry as captivating as the natural beauty that surrounds them, the people of the US Virg Islands are a dazzling reflection the continents from which they hail. A colourful community of Africans, East Indians, Jews, Arabs, Dominicans, French and Americans, the populace all sha a great affinity as Virgin Islande while still retaining their unique cultural differences.

Significantly, the majority of Virgin Islanders are descended from the Asante, Ibo, Mandika and Woloff tribes who were originally brought from West Africa's Gold Coast as slaves, and it is, perhaps, their tradition which linger most in the memor of the visitor.

Throughout the islands, and bor from a legacy of African fables and European "yarn spinning", storytellers weave their spells through dramatic verse, ancestral rhythms and flamboyant gestures. They are seen as caretakers of a rich oral lture that has survived for any generations.

awn from all ranks of the mmunity, the modern-day oryteller still regularly tertains at local cultural events, scinating local children with the isadventures of characters ch as "Anansi the Trickster" epicted as a man or spider), hose origins reach back to the bles brought from the Ashanti ople of West Africa. The slave mmunity, far from their meland and colourful aditions, felt that they existed a life of despair and hope- ssness and the Anansi stories ere told to help them find a way ut of problems, even when they ere seemingly insurmountable.

the evening, usually on the ght of the clear full moon, the aves would gather in the 'big rd' (the communal courtyard ea amid the rowhouse ructures where they lived) and ten to the storyteller – usually older and respected member the community – spin his tales. e stories were told with great ssion and sometimes even th energetic singing and ncing," says Glenn Davis, Chief esearcher with the Virgin ands Legislature and a master oryteller himself.

The storyteller would also tell *jumbi* (ghost) stories, which were cautionary tales that served to control the behaviour of young members of the community and impart certain values to them.

Even after slavery ended, storytelling continued to be an important part of island tradition. It helped to keep the fabric of the community strong by providing an arena in which to air problems or grievances, deal with concerns and provide solutions to various dilemmas or anxieties.

"Tim-Tim Time" is the phrase used by storytellers who customarily gather beneath the shade of a tree to introduce folk tales that educate as well as entertain. Evidence of this vibrant oral tradition can also be found in collections such as *Tales of the Immortelles* and other literary works that have preserved some

Opposite: "Don't Touch the Clouds" – a fabulous pastel and acrylic work by Janet Cook-Rutnik. Below: "Who Do Voodoo", an extraordinary work also by Janet Cook-Rutnik who is based at Guavaberry Farm on St. John.

a West African religion called *obi*. Many claim that it no longer exists, while most will agree that its power is limited to that segment of the population who believe in it.

Obeah potions are said to invest individuals with the power to succeed in one's endeavours and give control over others. Quite a few men are alleged to have been tricked into marriage after unwittingly consuming the "come-to-me sauce", which makes its victim irresistibly attracted to the woman who slipped it into his food. Wives are also known to have given their husbands "stay-at-home sauce" to curtail extra-marital philandering! In 1940, *The American Weekly* carried an account of obeah in the Virgin Islands and in 1944 – during the early days of tourism – a book entitled *The Virgin Islands and Their People* was banned for discussing the practice. Today, few Virgin Islanders will openly

acknowledge obeah, but, in practice, it is not unusual for children who misbehave to be coerced by adults with threats of an impending visit and subsequent capture by the dreaded *jumbies*. A person, when faced with an unfortunate situation or ailment, may attribute it to the performance of obeah by another. Likewise, power shortages or anything that goes awry is often blamed on the intervention of mischievous or evil spirits.

It is not exceptional to hear rumours of werewolves and other creatures who prowl the tropical night, such as the legendary horseshoe-shod "Cowfoot Woman" who, according to superstition, lurks along forested roadsides in vampiric apprehension, awaiting human prey!

In any event, superstition still flourishes to the extent that, on asking a local how he is doing, he is likely to respond "Not so good as you" – to avoid drawing attention to good fortune that, allegedly, tempts the spirits.

Above: "The Past Is Always Present", by Janet Cook-Rutnik depicts the ever-present influence of past cultures in the life of the Virgin Islanders.

of the Caribbean's best-loved stories. Of course, not all folk tales are fiction. Popular among islanders are the exploits of real-life Tortola strongman, Joseph "Tampo" Fahie, which served as inspiration for the contemporary series documented by Dr. Gilbert Sprauve of the University of the Virgin Islands.

A legacy of the African heritage – and distinct from the voodoo tradition – is *obeah* , a cultural belief in spirits, love potions, charms, herbs and the power of witchcraft – both good and bad – practised by obeah men. The practice is believed to stem from

Music and Dance

The music and dance of the Virgin Islands is a confluence of Caribbean, African and South American traditions. The sensuous and exotic *samba* hails from Brazil, while from Cuba comes the vibrant *conga*, *mambo*, *rumba*, *bolera* and *cha-cha*. Also fashionable among Virgin Islanders of Dominican descent is the unmistakable *merengue*. While Virgin Islanders of Hispanic birthright have proudly adopted merengue as their own, they also sway to the Latin beat of *salsa*, *jibaro* (country music) and the *plena*. The plena is inherently Puerto Rican, incorporating lyrics that highlight society's foibles. Famously, Spanish melodies have also infected calypso, especially the Christmas music called *parang*, performed with the guitar, ukelele and mandolin.

Indeed, music takes many forms in the Virgin Islands, from Afro-Caribbean-inspired rhythms and "talking drums" that echo the heartbeat of humanity, to sultry jazz melodies at local clubs and the annual St. Croix Jazz and Caribbean Music and Art Festival.

Right: The music and dance of the US Virgin Islands reflects the traditions of the Caribbean, Africa and South America.

Importantly, and reflecting the islands' strong African heritage, are those extemporaneous musical forms adapted from the ancient Ashanti tradition, like *cariso*, *bamboula* and *quelbe*. It is this music which is so ingrained and cherished in the hearts of the islanders and has kept tradition alive for generations. According to Glenn "Kwabena" Davis, who is assembling the first Virgin Islands music archive, messages hidden in cariso songs spread news from plantation to plantation. A clandestine form of

communication, cariso was used to convey strategy when African slaves fought for improved labour conditions and, ultimately, freedom. There is evidence that the song relay-system even supported the effort for freedom of the press. Cariso is alive today through the dedication of many tradition-bearers like Leona Watson and Cariso Singers from St. Croix. Like cariso, bamboula was accompanied by congas, maracas and other percussion instruments and used symbolism in its lyrics to galvanise protest.

With topics dealing with everything from current events, marital infidelity and rum-smuggling to society's ills, the colourful music form known as quelbe both entertains and educates. The "wash pan an' piece of stick" instrument of neighbouring Tortola's Elmo and the Sparkplugs is pure quelbe, a music presently enjoying a major revival through the annual Quelbe Music Festival.

Above and opposite: Cultural extravaganzas are held at the Reichhold Centre of Arts on St. Thomas.

Tracing its origins to Africa and evolving into an art form in Trinidad and Tobago, calypso (from the Hausa word *kaiso*) has now usurped quelbe as the islands' most popular music. Although there has been much debate over the origins of its name, many believe it derives from the Greek nymph, Calypso meaning "one who conceals".

In 1945, the Andrews Sisters' hit song *Rum and Coca-Cola* gave many Americans their first taste of commercialised calypso, although it was adapted from a satirical Trinidadian version concerning prostitution!

Booming from car radios and erupting from local bandstands, it is difficult not to be seduced by the pulsating beat of calypso. Visitors, however, may fail to catch the nuances of the double-edged lyrics which are infused with everything from gossip, scandal and politics to positive social messages.

Improvisation is the measure of the true calypsonian. Like the African-inspired cariso and bamboula, calypso carries the voice of its people – so much so that it has often functioned as the newspaper of the common man. During Carnival,

competitions among poetic calypsonians have given rise to new generation of artists with something to sing about. Additionally, reggae, originating from Jamaica, and soca – a spirited fusion of traditional calypso and soul music – is also greatly appreciated here.

Unique to the Caribbean, "scratch" bands produce their spontaneous and distinctive, live music by scratching on ridged gourds with wire, accompanied the flute, ukelele or guitar. Contemporary scratch bands utilise ingenious instruments fashioned from car exhaust pipe wash tubs and even bottles – producing a sound that ranges from high-pitched to deeply resonant. Once the primary entertainment at weddings and Christmas such bands can still b heard at quadrille performances

Interestingly, the electrifying sound of metal percussion instruments evolved from early street bands in Trinidad that bea steel rods against brake drums, buckets and even garbage can lids. The only musical instrumen to be invented in the 20th century, the steel pan was hammered from oil drums secur from US military bases in Trinida during World War II.

though Virgin Islanders demonstrably love their high-energy, "jump-up" and dance music, spiritual hymns are also heard in places of worship. Particularly moving is the Caribbean Choral's annual performance of Handel's *Messiah*, together with Catholic and Protestant hymns sung in calypso cadence. It is redolent of the European colonial era.

Virgin Islanders will dance to celebrate virtually any occasion with an exuberance and vitality that overwhelmingly surpasses mere recreation. Few other art forms express their mood, temperament or cultural heritage adequately. African slaves, uprooted from their motherland, also imported their dance traditions with them. Modern Virgin Islanders can thank their ancestors who adapted formal square-dance steps from European plantation ballrooms, adding an African drum beat to produce quadrille. Venerated for its sophisticated hip-swaying, full-spirited softness and its reverberating melodies played on the flute, ukelele and banjo, the quadrille is regarded by many as the first native dance of the Virgin Islands. Traditionally-adorned quadrille performers such as the

St. Croix and the St. John Heritage Dancers and Mongo Niles Cultural Dancers have succeeded in reviving intricate plantation-era modified minuets, Austrian waltzes and even the spirited polka.

One dance that has recovered from near-extinction is the bamboula, whose primaeval rhythms and trilling flutes so terrified the white planters that the dance was forbidden. Fortunately, groups like the Joseph Gomez Macislin Bamboula Dance Company, which is composed of schoolgirls in swirling petticoats, are regenerating an enthusiastic revival of this energetic, sensual dance form.

Visitors in search of colourful entertainment might plan to catch a performance by the Pistarckle Theatre, or visit the Maho Bay Performing Arts Pavilion on St. John.

For the last 20 years, the Reichhold Centre for the Arts on St. Thomas has been a premier cultural centre in the Caribbean. Set within lush tropical gardens, this state-of-the-art 1,200-seat amphitheatre on Brewer's Bay plays host to a regular array of events and exhibits that promote

and stimulate the US Virgin Island's unique Caribbean culture.

Here, visitors can enjoy performances by some of the finest ballet companies, chorale and repertory groups in the world. The venue often features cultural extravaganzas with exotically beautiful costumes and exhilarating choreography in a kaleidoscope of music and dance.

St. Croix's Island Centre attracts top names to its 600-seat theatre and open-air amphitheatre that accommodates 1,600 people.

chitecture

eclectic mix of architecture
ands as testament to the
ands' history where,
markably structures have
thstood the various influences
Danish and German settlers,
ench refugees, pirates, slaves
d military forces. The rolling
ndscape is sprinkled with
toric ruins where the subtle
ash of pastels and the contrast
vivid terra cotta blend subtly.

St. Thomas you will see the
nish and English influence
dent both in modest store
nts and grandiose mansions
spectively. On St. Croix one can
ur the well-preserved historical
ntres of Christiansted and
ederiskted, where the
aracter of the islands'
chitecture is well-exemplified.
ost of the buildings in
ristiansted are 18th- or 19th-
ntury Danish: cream coloured
th red roofs and shady arcades
d galleries. The town was
unded in 1734 and is no ill-
anned tangle, but rather a
ructured grid of streets with
non-tinted Fort Christiansvaern
its focus.

aditional buildings in the US
rgin Islands are usually no
gher than two floors, with the

ground floor being used as a shop
or workshop and the upper floor
as living quarters. The ground
floor walls were constructed of
masonry to counter the risk of
fire, and the upper part of the
building was traditionally built of
wood. There are often shady
galleries round the upper floor,
sometimes extending over the
pavement in front of the house,
supported by columns, providing
an inviting, cool arcade beneath.

Frederiksted, nestled on a bay at
the west end of St Croix has
many examples of traditional
architecture. Many buildings are
decorated with jig-sawed

"carpenter's lace" and the
symmetric two-storey frame
houses on Queen Street are
typical of the architecture that
gives the town its characteristic
Victorian flavour. This elegant
gingerbread trim is mainly
attached to the galleries of
buildings and is complemented
by charming wooden ballusters.
A pleasing feature, it is often
further enchanced by ornate
wooden porches.

*The architecture of the US Virgin Islands
has been strongly influenced by its Danish
and English heritage – particularly in area
like Christiansted and Frederiksted on St.
Croix. Below: The red-roofed waterfront
buildings of Charlotte Amalie.*

festival

The US Virgin Islands are host to many spectacular festiva throughout the year. Should your visit coincide with one, the experience will give your trip an extra dimension and leave you with an unforgettable impressio of the sheer energy and vitality of the islanders themselves.

Don't worry about securing a costume – all you need is a willi spirit and a desire to party late into the night.

The season opens with the **St. Croix Blues and Heritage Festiv** which is held in late January. Fans of this musical style will fin this event to be the treat of a lifetime. Blues artists converge from the national and local scenes to play at various locations across St. Croix.

A few weeks later, following in proud American tradition, is the **St. Patrick's Day** celebrations – an inter-island affair held on the nearest Saturday to 17th March culminating in a splendid parade

The main event, however, is the spectacular **St. Thomas Carniva**

Left: Revellers wearing brightly-coloured costumes celebrate and party during the Carnival parade on St. John. Opposite: Th costumes worn during the Carnival parad on St. Thomas are usually made up in a host of dazzling and iridescent fabrics.

nd events

e Caribbean's second-largest
tural festival, the Carnival is
ficially celebrated during the
st two weeks of April, although
e opening festivities begin
eeks earlier. A month-long
ries of glittering pageants and
ent shows at Lionel Roberts
adium select candidates for the
een of Carnival and the King of
e Band, whose coronations are
d in Emancipation Garden and
e followed by the formal
niversary Ball. Nightly concerts
own as the Calypso
minations present a musical
ash between local calypso-king
pefuls. At the Junior Calypso
mpetition, the voice of youth
gs out loud and clear through
rformers like the Mighty Simba
d Lady Charlotte, whose witty
ics often poke fun at adult
bles. Vying for the honour tobe
e King and Queen, participants
rade in magnificent costumes
at will later form the
nterpieces of parade troupes.
e traditional stilt-walkers
noco jumbies), who are the
nbodiment of terror and joy for
y Virgin Islands child, dance to
e inspired beat of the steel
um. Dressed in bright
escent colours, usually with
rrors sewn into their
stumes, it is an incredible sight
watch these talented

performers on 12-foot (4-metre)
stilts whirling and gliding while
the music builds up to a
thunderous crescendo. Legend
tells that these spirits were
invisible, which is why they wear
mirrors: all you see when you
look at a *moco jumbie* is a
reflection of yourself!

Market Fair, an eclectic mix of
ethnic foods and colourful
displays of arts and crafts,
signals the countdown to the
main celebrations. Held in
Rothschild Francis Market Square
which is lined with stalls selling

tasty food around the clock, the
food-fest caters to even the
most discerning palate with a
fantastic spread of native
delicacies, including saltfish, flaky
patties, stewed tamarind and
potato stuffing. Stalls selling
home-made pastries, candles and
drinks sit side-by-side with those
selling locally-grown plants,
exotic fruits and fragrant spices.
Women sporting "market lady"
skirts and headscarves chop
sticks of sugar cane. Nightly
entertainment can range from
the incredible sounds of live

nds to groups of friends
nking a delicious, but potent,
x of rum and coconut milk.

e Virgin Islands Calypso
mpetition follows the Market
ir and features the talents of
al calypsonians battling it out
a contest of wit and lyric. The
gins of calypso are in the slave
ngs brought by Africans to the
est Indies in the 17th century.
e slaves brought two distinct
pes of music: work songs and
ald songs. The work songs
ere sung to lift the spirit and
ere usually laments on the
rdships they suffered. The
hter, satirical songs were like
e social commentaries that are
cognisable of today's calypso.
e sound of the words is as
portant as the words
emselves; with double
eanings, expressive folk
yings and stories told with
eat gesturing and emotion.

e official opening of Carnival
gins with the dedication of
rnival Village. For many the real
lebrations start with what they
gard as the most popular

event, the pre-dawn festivies
along waterfront known as the
J'Ouvert Morning Tramp
(meaning "the opening of the
day"), which heralds the arrival
of the parades. Moved by
sensual rhythms and the
warming rays of the rising sun,
thousands of revellers snake
their way along the roads
dancing behind blaring bands on
brightly-decorated flatbed trucks.
Wearing sneakers, T-shirts, glitter
and sometimes little else,
whistle-blowing dancers all try to
out-perform each other in the
spirit of outrageous
fun. Needless to say,
the *J'Ouvert* parade is
not for the faint-
hearted.

The pace picks up
progressively as
powerboats and
traditional wooden
bateaux race on the
Charlotte Amalie
waterfront. Once the
calypso crown has
been bestowed, the
Calypso Revue
serves as an
international
showcase for rival
calypsonians to
exchange quips and
risqué lyrics.

The steel pan reigns supreme at
Pan-O-Rama where visitors can
dance to the liquid sounds of the
Rising Stars Steel Orchestra.
Lovers of the big-band sound
pack Lionel Roberts Stadium for
the Brass-O-Rama competition,
where Mandingo Brass, Jam
Band and Milo and the Kings play
long into the night.

The Adults Parade takes centre
stage on the final day in a
showcase of spectacular
costumes made from glittering
lamé fabrics decorated with

ostrich plumes, pearls and peacock feathers. Troupes (clubs) with as many as 500 members transform themselves into African tribesmen, Samurai warriors, giant flowers, musical instruments and other surreal creatures that defy the imagination. They spend weeks choreographing intricate and inspired dance steps to accompany their chosen band. An all-day event that often continues long after sunset, the parade is a seemingly endless procession of imaginative creations, a symphony of sight and sound that closes with the traditional troupe of clowns, Indians and Zulu warriors.

St. Thomas is ready to breathe a sigh of relief and get some sleep by the time the dazzling "Thunder over Charlotte Amalie" firework display heralds the end of yet another carnival and the stroke of midnight closes the Carnival Village.

The **Fourth of July Celebration**, held on St. John is the only Virgin Islands carnival held in

Top: Traditional moco jumbies dance to the inspired beat of the steel drum. Left: Fourth of July celebrations on St. John. Opposite top: The costumes worn during the Carnival parade on St. Thomas are hand-made and ornately decorated. Opposite: Smiling teenager enjoys the Carnival parade.

Festival, which is held over two weeks in October with colourful music, arts and cultural exhibits.

Late December heralds the much-awaited **Crucian Christmas Festival**. Held at the Island Center for the Performing Arts, the Miss St. Croix Pageant opens the two-week celebrations, which begin in late-December and last until Epiphany. Noted for its stunning and talented ladies, St. Croix Pageant winners have often gone on to international competitions. St. Croix's Food Fair takes place in both Frederiksted and Christiansted, where local delicacies like callaloo, conch and saltfish can be found in nearly every booth. The largest of the US Virgin Islands, St. Croix traditionally hosts Festival Villages at both ends of the island.

The Children's Parade dances through historic Christiansted on its way to the wharf. Boasting over 40 resplendent troupes and floats, the splendid Adult Parade snakes it way down King Street in Frederiksted for the finale of the Crucian Christmas Festival. So dazzling are the colours of their costumes that many of St. Croix's Adult

Parade troupes, like Sanchez and Associates, have waiting lists of new-member hopefuls.

With its strong French heritage, the term *babooshay* (meaning "live it up") is appropriate to describe St. Croix's special spirit of sheer abandon. Where else in the world can you find a local senator dancing in the middle of the street dressed in a silver lamé jumpsuit or toga?

njunction with America's dependence Day. Smaller in pulation than St. Thomas or . Croix, St. John compensates involving a larger cross-ction of locals, whose floats splay a wit peculiar to St. hnians. Revellers in Cruz Bay n stop at the Food Fair to eat a ntastic array of traditonal and foods, drink and make erry in the greased pole ntests and bun-on-a-string ces. As a final salute to the urth of July and the spirit of rnival, a brilliant display of eworks lights up Cruz Bay.

. Croix is host to another music stival in its **St. Croix Jazz and aribbean Music and Arts**

shop til.

ANTIQUE ALLEY

JADE WRAPS

FAT TUESDAYS

Shady Day

ou drop

You do not have to be a pirate to pick up some valuable booty on a shopping trip to e US Virgin Islands. St. Thomas a veritable treasure trove of orld class riches, all at rock ottom duty-free prices. Treat ourself – after all a vacation is ot complete without some ssential retail therapy. As you rowse the stores on St. homas, you will find it hard to sist the offers found in the undreds of shops that line harlotte Amalie's waterfront. t. Thomas provides fabulous hopping opportunities and you ill find yourself in shopping eaven, unearthing buried easure at unbelievably low ices. The biggest savings are liquor, cameras and ectronics, perfumes and osmetics, fashions, linens, hina and crystal and, of course, wellery and watches. Many ores also stock a wonderful nge of local gift items, hand-afted jewellery and arts and afts. (For further information, e Culture Club page 96.)

otographs clockwise from top left: Best Both Worlds Gallery on St. John sells a zzling range of jewellery, sculptures and e art; the waterfront on St. Thomas is a rynth of narrow alleys; the Donald nnell Gallery on St. John produces a vast ay of pottery and gift items; Mongoose nction on St. John; Shady Days stocks an cellent range of designer sunglasses.

A.H. Riise Gift & Liquor Store
37 Main Street, Tel: 776-2303

The US Virgin Islands' oldest, largest and most complete duty-free gift and liquor store is located in a series of beautifully restored, brick and stonework, 19th-century Danish warehouses that stretch from Charlotte Amalie's Main Street to the waterfront. The store, which was established in 1838, is a highlight for all visitors to St. Thomas.

Within the complex is St. Thomas' oldest and largest perfumery, selling virtually every fragrance imaginable – from the timeless classics to the newest designer scents – and all at substantial savings.

A.H. Riise also has a fabulous selection of spirits and tobaccos at savings of up to 50 per cent on high street prices. They also sell a vast collection of Caribbean rums, single malt whiskies and vintage premium liqueurs. This is the best place to find the island's widest selection of cigars, all displayed in a walk-in humidor.

A selection of the finest brand-name jewellery – including Tiffany and Co. – is the highlight of the extensive selection at A.H. Riise. The store is the Virgin Islands' only authorised agent for Rolex watches, and there is also a fine selection of Swiss watches available. Speciality boutiques offer a collection of loose diamonds, tanzanite and emerald jewellery. There is also a platinum boutique and an outlet for rare ancient coins.

The A.H. Riise Mall is also home to speciality stores, such as the **Linen House**, **Speedo Fitness**, **Pusser's Company Store**, **Little Switzerland**, **Colombian Emeralds International** and the alfresco **Café Amici**.

Little Switzerland is located here and is the only outlet on St. Thomas for Baccarat and Waterford crystal. Rosenthal dinnerware and gifts are also on sale here, as well as Crabtree and Evelyn products. A boutique selling fashion jewellery, leather goods and accessories is worth a visit. **Colombian Emeralds International** is the leading emerald jeweller in the Caribbean and offers a wide selection of Colombian emeralds, along with diamonds, precious gemstones and fine Italian gold jewellery.

The staff are knowledgeable and multi-lingual and for convenience they will deliver purchases to your cruise ship or the airport on St. Thomas.

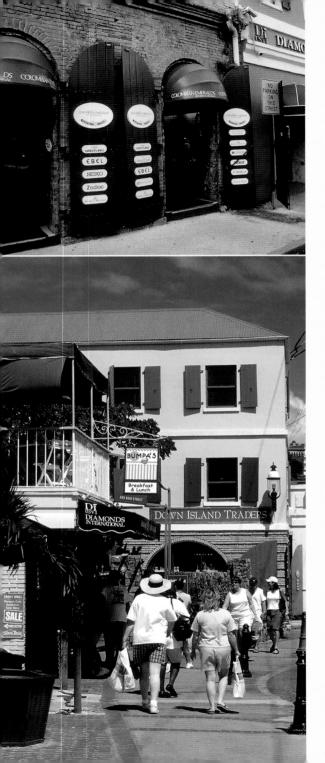

A Chew or Two
Trompeter Gade, Tel: 774-6675

Chocoholics can relax in the knowledge that their every wish can be granted at this fabulous store which specialises in Godiva chocolate and truffles. Their selection of truffles is vast and the only problem is choosing between the trays of temptation laid before you. They also sell Godiva coffee, gourmet jelly beans and West Indian jellies.

Amsterdam Sauer
Main Street, Tel: 774-2222;
Havensight Mall, Tel: 776-3828;
The Ritz Carlton, Tel: 779-2308

Amsterdam Sauer has been a direct source for jewellery and gems since 1941. Since then three generations of the Sauer family have collaborated with world-renowned designers and jewellers to produce a unique collection of fine jewellery. The stores in St. Thomas offer the largest selection of unset gems in the Caribbean at great prices. Ask to see the Imperial Topaz collection – the supply of this stone will soon be exhausted.

Top: Charlotte Amalie is home to a fantastic selection of jewellery stores all offering precious and semi-precious stones at rock-bottom duty-free prices. Bottom: Down Island Traders is an authentic market that carries a fascinating choice of gift and souvenir items.

Artistic Jewellers
32 Main Street, Tel: 776-3299
or 1-800 653-3113

One of the oldest and most reputable stores on the island, Artistic offers a fabulous selection of fine quality necklaces, bracelets, bangles, earrings and watches. They are the authorised dealer for many reputable names, including the Blue Lagoon cultured pearls by Mikimoto. Precious and semi-precious stones are sold here, including diamonds, emeralds, rubies, and sapphires.

Boolchands
9B Main Street, Tel: 776-8550;
31 Main Street, Tel: 776-9674;
Havensight Mall, Tel: 776-0302

Boolchands has enjoyed a reputation as the region's largest retailer of photographic equipment for 60 years. They offer great prices on the latest cameras, hi-fi, video equipment and telephones. Boolchands' ne watch and gift section is now located in the Main Street store which also stocks a range of designer sunglasses, leather gif and accessories. Boolchands ha 17 shops throughout the Caribbean, and some gentle negotiation will usually guarante a better price.

ptain's Corner
ain Street, opposite H Stern,
l: 774-8435

cated at the
art of Main
reet for more
an 20 years,
sitors can
owse
rough the
rgest
lection of
ique souvenirs
d island crafts on
. Thomas. They stock
rimar jewellery, the gem of the
aribbean, sterling silver, shell
d coral jewellery. There is a
alk-in humidor with fine cigars,
well as a collection of colourful
shirts, hats and caps.

ardow
ain Street (two stores);
avensight Mall (two stores);
enchman's Reef (one store);
l: 776-1140/1-800-CARDOWS

ardow is justly famous for their
st selection of jewellery and
eir guarantee of prices up to 50
er cent lower than US mainland
ices. The Cardow family travels
over the world over
rchasing gemstones direct
om source, and their expert
signers create exclusive pieces
their own factory.

Carson Co. Antiques
Royal Dane Mall, Tel: 774-6175

Located at the north-west
end of Royal Dane
Mall, the two
rooms of
fascinating
antiquities
include some
rare books,
ancient coins,
African masks
and some
interesting books.

The Crystal Shoppe
14 Main Street, Tel: 777-9835

This family-run business
was founded in 1983 and
stocks some of the
world's finest crystal and
gift items. The duty-free
prices here offer
substantial savings over
US mainland prices.

Dazzlers Duty-free Shop
Havensight Mall,
Tel: 1-800-25-JEWEL

Dazzlers in Havensight Mall
sells a hugely discounted
selection of liquor, perfume,
jewellery, watches and
cigars. They boast the
largest walk-in humidor in
the Caribbean, with brands
from around the world.

Diamonds International (DIUSVI)
3a Main Street, Tel: 774-1516;
Havensight Mall, Tel: 776-0040;

Diamonds International stock a
vast selection of stones to suit
every requirement and pocket.
Over 2,000 diamonds are
displayed through the spectrum –
from blue-white, natural pink,
orange, yellow to mauve. Choose
your stone and setting, and
within one hour you will have
your own personalised article of
exquisite jewellery.

*Below: Brightly-coloured parrots are kept by
Shipwrecker's Antiques in Royal Dane Mall
on St. Thomas.*

Dockside Bookshop
Havensight Mall, Tel: 774-4937

This is the best book shop in the Virgin Islands, with a great selection of best-sellers, novels, travel and cookery books, as well as a wonderful choice of books on the Caribbean.

Down Island Trader's Boutique
West of Vendor's Plaza on the Waterfront. Tel: 776-4641

This store stocks a selection of locally-made children's gifts, T-shirts, speciality foods, spices, jellies, hot sauces, teas and

Above: Rio Cigars is an excellent place to find a wide range of imported cigars all kept in temperature-controlled humidors. Opposite: The interior of MAPes MONDe.

coffees, artwork, prints, books and music. This authentic market also carries a fascinating choice of colourful hand-painted Christmas decorations, water-colour maps of the West Indies, greetings cards, colourful beach wear and silver jewellery.

Drake's Passage Mall
Charlotte Amalie

Located two blocks from Emancipation Garden, this is the only air-conditioned mall in downtown Charlotte Amalie. This historic building, once a pier warehouse, now hosts more than 30 unique shops and the excellent *Hardwood Grill*. There is a huge choice of quality jewellery, leather goods, men's and women's clothing, perfumes, electronics, gifts and confectionery.

Local Color
Hibiscus Alley, Tel: 774-7327

Located halfway down Hibiscus Alley, this colourful store specialises in unique T-shirts and casual clothing for both children and adults. It is owned by artist Kerry Topper, who paints in the bright colours synonymous with her surroundings. She sells her work throughout the West Indies.

Mr. Tablecloth
6 Main Street, Tel: 774-4343

Mr. Tablecloth's original linen sto is devoted to selling tablecloths and accessories, place mats, doilies and aprons. The owner, Jeannie, travels regularly to Chi to find the best in quality and workmanship and imports tablecloths in all sizes and varie of fine fabrics. Mr. Tablecloth ha a firm price policy, so the saving are always unbelievable, with u to 70 per cent off US mainland prices. The range has recently expanded to include a lovely selection of bedroom linens.

MAPes MONDe
Main Street in the centre of the A.H. Riise building, Tel: 776-228

The MAPes MONDe Print Galler is a delightful shop with an extensive collection of high-qual reproduction and contemporary Caribbean art. They sell some limited edition tropical silk-scree and also publish rare West India images, maps and botanical illustrations printed on fine Italia pure linen rag and acid-free papers. Their collection of book is full of surprises, including the own edition of *Treasure Island*; a spell-binding account of the 173 slave rebellion on St. John in *Nig of the Silent Drums*, which is

ustrated with engravings by
illiam Blake; and a carefully-
esearched compilation of
xtracts from Christopher
olumbus' log in *Conquest of*
den 1493-1515. The latter was
ritten by the owner of MAPes
ONDe, Michael Paiwonsky who
tudied at the University of
hicago and the University of
dinburgh. In addition to his
xtensive first-hand experience,
e has served as a trustee of the
irgin Islands Archaeological
ociety and has lectured on
est Indian history throughout
e region

his store is a must for anybody
ith even a vague interest in the
story of the Virgin Islands – if
nly to browse through the rare
storical photographs depicting
e on the islands. MAPes MONDe
so have an outlet in Mongoose
unction on St. John.

icole Miller
alm Passage, Main Street,
el: 774-8286

icole Miller is world-renowned for
er fabulous silk items, including
oxer shorts, ties, bathrobes,
ckets, waistcoats and ladies
ear. This elegant store with its
arble floor and chic interior is a
eat place to find these classy
esigns at unbeatable prices.

Old Danish Warehouse
Grand Hotel, Tel: 774-8432

At this charming emporium,
located opposite the Post Office
in the historic Grand Hotel, you
can find something for everyone
without breaking your budget.
They sell T-shirts, souvenirs,
inexpensive jewellery fashioned
from silver, shells and coral, as
well as caps and casual wear.

Rio Cigars
Royal Dane Mall, Tel: 774-5877

This tranquil oasis amidst the
bustle of the shopping frenzy of
Charlotte Amalie is a delight –
even if you are not a cigar
aficionado. There is a large walk-

in humidor where an incredible
selection of cigars are on offer.
They also sell beautifully-crafted
humidors and there is a full bar
here, where shoppers can relax in
air-conditioned comfort.

Royal Caribbean
33 Main Street, Tel: 776-4110;
Havensight Mall, Tel: 776-8890

This is the largest camera and
electronics store in the Caribbean
and carries top-of-the-range
cameras, electronic items,
watches and jewellery at
discounted prices. The gift
department stocks luxury
products such as pens, lighters,
leather goods, watches and

Tanzanite International
Main Street,
Tel: 774-6181

This entire store is dedicated to the tanzanite gemstone. Here you can see the largest tanzanite stone in the West Indies, the 99-carat *Star of the Caribbean*, displayed in a special showcase.

Mongoose Junction
Cruz Bay, St. John

Mongoose Junction is a unique shopping complex set in the most unusual stone and timber buildings on the north end of Cruz Bay. This magnificent showpiece by local architect Glen Speer is a warren of buildings, stairways and archways built in coral, brick and Honduran mahogany. The shops are on different levels centrered around an open courtyard, where live music and good food is available each evening. It is a focal point of the island and offers dozens of fascinating shops, galleries, restaurants and cafés. Visitors can watch a number of artisans at work in their studios here. Gifts, jewellery and clothes from around the world are available.

sunglasses. Pearls, gold jewellery, African tanzanite, other precious stones and diamond jewellery are all on offer.

Rhiannonn's
Red Hook, Tel: 779-1877

This delightful New Age store sells a host of fascinating items, from sparkling fairy dust to hand-made quilts and wall-hangings by local artists. Other interesting

Above: Mongoose Junction is a unique shopping complex housing a collection of jewellery, arts and crafts, clothing and souvenir stores. Opposite: Pink Papaya sells a collection of wares painted in the bright colours synonymous with the Caribbean.

items including incense sticks, tarot cards, candles and a great selection of books. Silver and gold jewellery is also on offer.

Shipwrecker's Antiques
Royal Dane Mall, Tel: 774-2074

This is a delightful store with artwork and maps of the West Indies hung around the exposed brick walls. They stock ship wheels, compasses, lanterns and antique pieces of boats collected by the owner who also works in the salvage business. An interesting selection of books, old coins and prints are for sale.

Best of Both Worlds
*Mongoose Junction, Cruz Bay,
St. John. Tel: 693-7005*

This fabulous gallery features a
magnificent selection of oil and
water-colour paintings, metal and
wire sculptures, jewellery and
sparkling waterfalls. They
represent the works of a number
of local artists, and the airy
upstairs floor is a veritable
treasure trove of interesting
crafts and souvenirs.

Island Made
*Palm Plaza, Southshore Road,
Cruz Bay, St. John, Tel: 693-7575*

Search out some authentic
craftsmanship and add some
local flavour to your shopping.
Original fine arts and artefacts –
pottery, masks, stained glass,
ornaments, beaded jewellery –
are displayed in this air-
conditioned gallery. Work for sale
is produced by a co-operative of
local island artisans.

Donald Schnell Studio
*Mongoose Junction, Cruz Bay,
St. John, Tel: 253-7107*

This fascinating studio produces
a wealth of custom-made
pottery, including wall sconces,
wind chimes, photo frames,
candlesticks and hanging
lanterns. The pottery is all
produced in the studio where
visitors can spend many hours
browsing through the vast
selection of gift items on sale.
Treat yourself to a Donald Schnell
fountain made up of richly
coloured pottery towers – the
perfect gift for the world-weary
executive in need of a little
relaxing water therapy.

Pink Papaya
*In the centre of Cruz Bay near to
Chase Bank, Tel: 693-8535*

This dazzling shop stocks a vast
range of artwork, home
furnishings, linens, dinnerware,
ceramics and stained glass – all in
vivid tropical colours. They also
stock a selection of books on the
West Indies and prints by local
and international artists.

Shady Days
Cruz Bay, Tel: 693-7625

The best source for cigars on the
tiny island of St. John and a great
place to find a fantastic collection
of designer sunglasses.The
cigars are imported from around
the world and a selection of
humidors are also on sale.

The US Virgin Islands is home to a fantastic choice of bars ranging from cosy intimate settings that offer fine wines and champagne to fun-filled establishments serving lethal cocktails along with loud and lively entertainment.

ST. THOMAS

A short walk around Charlotte Amalie on St. Thomas will reveal some great places to drink including **Hotel 1829**. The elegant dark bar with its stone floor and walls is a cool, comfortable place to relax and enjoy a wide range of French and New World wines, as well as ever-changing daily appetizers. There are also backgammon tables for those looking for a sporting challenge.

The **Greenhouse** on the Waterfront provides a totally different atmostphere and is one of the main dance spots on the island. There are competitions throughout the week, as well as sporting events, pool and foozba tables. The restaurant serves great snacks including pizzas and barbecue specials.

Virgillio's Wine Cellar is an elegant establishment with a long mahogany bar, sparkling chandeliers and intimate booths or tables. There is a selection of over 450 wines in the cellar, a large number of which are served by the glass. There is also a pianist on Thursday, Friday and Saturday evenings.

Leaving Charlotte Amalie in the direction of Frenchtown leads to **Epernay** – a dark and cosy bistro and bar with a fine selection of champagne and Old and New World wines. The bar, which is a magnet for the 'in crowd' on St. Thomas, offers a tasty selection of snacks and sushi.

et uncorked

Alexander's Bar is a great place if you are looking for a watering hole to catch up on the latest sporting events and drink ice-cold beers in a convivial atmosphere.

At Bluebeard's Castle, **Room with a View** with its floor-to-ceiling windows affords fantastic views of the harbour and Charlotte Amalie. This is an especially lovely place to watch the sunset. The wine list is excellent and there is a daily list of appetizers.

In Red Hook, **Duffy's Love Shack** is a fun place which serves exotic cocktails and ice-cold beers to the sounds of loud music. Dancing features on certain evenings throughout the week.

ST. JOHN

In St. John, look no further than the **Dockside Pub** right beside the ferry dock where ice-cold beers and tasty snacks are served.

A short walk down into Cruz Bay leads to **J.J.s Texas Coast Café** which again serves ice-cold beers and tasty cocktails on a shady terrace. They serve a selection of Tex/Mex dishes including chilli, enchiladas and fried cheese.

Morgan's Mango is an open-air pink and turquoise restaurant overlooking Cruz Bay. They serve contemporary blend of

Caribbean fare that features some tastebud-sharpening spices and robust flavours. The pre-dinner cocktail menu is particularly worthy of note.

Pusser's Pub in the Wharfside Village is decorated in a nautical theme and is a great spot to relax and chat with local folk.

In Coral Bay, **Skinny Legs Bar and Restaurant** is a casual al fresco spot which serves great sandwiches and barbecued dishes. The beers are cold and the atmosphere lively – particularly on a Friday evening when there is usually a live band.

ST. CROIX

St. Croix offers some fun drinking establishments including the pretty setting of **Duggan's Reef** which is popular with both holidaymakers and locals. Its breezy veranda overlooks Buck Island and they also serve great international dishes.

At **Cane Bay** there is a beach bar which is situated close to the water. They serve snacks as well as excellent seafood and steaks.

On the west coast just north of Frederiksted, the **Rainbow Beach Club** is situated on a fabulous stretch of white sand and is packed with a lively crowd at

weekends. They serve cheap snacks and great cocktails.

At **Chenay Bay** there is a tiny beach bar which serves cold beers and delicious snacks. This is a great place to revive the spirit after battling the waves on a windsurfing mission!

Whatever your choice for the locale or atmosphere of your preferred watering hole, you are sure to be spoiled for choice on the islands. Whether you are dreaming of romantic cocktails beneath a starry moonlit sky, or a bustling party atmostphere with dancing into the small hours, the place of your choice is here to be discovered.

eat you

eart out

he US Virgin Islands' cultural heritage and the influence of settlers in the region oughout the centuries can be asurably encountered through e legacy of their cuisine. The nish influence survives in rious dishes. Their love of tter, for instance, has filtered wn into Caribbean cooking and e islands pioneered the eparation of conch in butter uce. *Frikadellar* is a dish of ditional Danish meatballs made m a combination of pork and al. Another local delicacy made m marinating herring, as well boiled or Danish baked ham aces many tables. For those h a sweet tooth, Danish sserts such as red grout – ade of guava or red prickly pear it juice – and almond *kranse* ke is similarly evocative of the nsk days.

en the European settlers ived in the late 17th century d began to import slaves from st Africa. African culture was en blended with various ropean customs to oduce traditional West

otographs clockwise from top left: islands' cuisine draws its inspiration n abundant fresh produce; ical local fruits; fresh lobster is gular feature on most menus; food dishes are served in many cious sauces. Right: A rare iguana!

Indian dishes. It is overwhelmingly evident in local foods such as fungi (pastry cornmeal), goat water (goat soup), souse (pig's head soup with lime juice), johnny cakes (fried bread) and maubi (tonic made from maubi tree bark with other herbs). Local vegetables such as callaloo and okra, and fruits like mango and papaya are also a staple ingredient in many local dishes.

Seafood is, of course, extremely important to the gastronomy of the US Virgin Islands. Famous for its beautiful shell and succulent meat, the queen conch is a local delicacy. Sliced thin and marinated in lime juice, conch salad can be served as an appetiser, ground and combined with savoury vegetables Creole-style over rice as a main meal, or used in chowder and fried fritters.

The Hispanic heritage survives in beef stew and roast pork dishes and the Caribbean cousin of the Mexican burrito made from goat, shrimp or chicken instead of beans and beefs, the roti retains its taste even when served cold. Some of the best recipes for this flat-bread envelope stuffed with curried meat and served with mango chutney, migrated from Trinidad and Tobago. The Portuguese, too, have contributed a splash of the Mediterranean in garlic pork, fava bean and saltfish dishes.

Other cultures in the modern US Virgin Islands are represented through their cooking. One can sample world-class French, Italian, Chinese, Indian dishes and more. The cuisine is rated amongst the best in the world with some excellent restaurants to sample.

In the winter season, reservations are recommended for all restaurants, with the exception of the most casual lunch or breakfast spots. The larger your party, the more likely a reservation will limit your wait. Most restaurants accept Master Card, Visa and Amex, but do check in advance.

ST. THOMAS

Craig and Sally's
Tel: 340-779-9949

Located in Frenchtown, this excellent restaurant is run by owners Craig and Sally, and together they provide superb service in a centrally-located spot. The food is an imaginative and artistic blend of traditional European and modern Caribbean and is always fresh and bursting with flavour. A feeling of confidence underlies such dishes as tender beef fillet stuffed with blue cheese, polenta-crusted snapper with artichoke sauce or swordfish marinated in lime juice and local spices. An excellent selection of wines always includes champagnes, French and New World bins. Closed Monday and Tuesday. (*Moderate to expensive*)

Virgillio's
Tel: 340-776-4920

This cosy restaurant on Back Street has a charming atmosphere and diners can expect to sample some refined up-to-date north Italian cooking. An eclectic blend of artworks and

Top: Excellent cuisine is served on board day cruises around the islands. Centre: The elegant Hotel 1829. Bottom: Fresh local peppers are a feature of many dishes.

prints line the two-storey brick walls and the staff are always welcoming and friendly. An impressive range of fresh pasta dishes are served in delicious sauces, as well as traditional fa such as veal saltimboca, eggpla parmigiana or cappellini with a zesty vodka sauce. The daily specials include fresh seafood and meat options. Reservations are a must. Closed on Sunday. (*Moderate to expensive*)

Herve's
Tel: 340-777-9703

This charming hillside restaurar affords wonderful views of Charlotte Amalie and serves some of the finest cuisine to be found in the islands. They have kept ahead of the times and created a contemporary menu that juxtaposes culinary culture from traditional French to modern American. Dishes inclu sesame-crusted tuna served in piquant ginger sauce or char-grilled shrimp flavoured with papaya and mango. Meat dishe are expertly cooked in fragrant herbs and spices and the wine list boasts a varied choice ranging from sunny New World whites to serious red Bordeaux and burgundies. Reservations recommended for evenings. (*Expensive*)

tel 1829
: 340-776-1829

e excellent reputation of this
ohisticated menu has made
s establishment a favourite of
th locals and visitors to St.
omas. Exquisite food,
mbined with an *al fresco*
ndlelit setting and excellent
rvice are all hallmarks of this
toric landmark. The creative
hes are superbly-presented
d include a wonderful selection
locally-grown and imported
oduce, all served in a classical,
t innovative style. Beluga and
vruga caviar is also available
d served with blinis and sour
eam. Reservations are
commended. Closed on
nday. *(Expensive)*

ady's Cafe
: 340-774-6604

s charming air-conditioned
tery is set amidst the old
arehouses of Royal Dane Mall
d serves good value tasty
hes including a selection of
stas, sandwiches and tasty
rgers. The menu includes a
ection of excellent West Indian
hes which make a delicious
ernative to the international
re. Try a bottle of Gladys'
icious (but spicy) hot sauce!
expensive)

Eunice's Terrace
Tel: 340-775-3975

This busy two-storey restaurant
is located near to the
Renaissance Beach Resort and
serves an exciting menu where
traditional West Indian cuisine is
served in a quaint setting. Eunice
has a reputation for cooking the
best conch on the island. It is
delicious either served in a
piquant lime juice and butter
sauce or fried in a light batter
into fritters. Her calalloo soup
(made from local spinach and
seafood) is fabulous and an
evening here makes for a unique
eating experience. Closed for
Sunday lunch. *(Inexpensive)*

ST. JOHN

Uncle Joe's Barbecue

This brightly-painted shack is
situated directly on Cruz Bay
ferry port and serves fabulous
barbecued food. Chicken or pork
is slowly roasted for ninety
minutes in the oven and then
seared on a black steel drum and
flavoured with a zesty barbeque
sauce. The resulting melt-in-the-
mouth meat is served up with
rice, beans and corn on the cob.
This is one of the best informal
eating experiences on the island
served up by some truly
charming staff. *(Inexpensive)*

Sputnick's

On East End Road in Coral Bay
just before Skinny Legs Bar,
Sputnick's serves delicious and
hearty breakfasts. The interior is
furnished with high wooden
tables painted in bright Caribbean
tones and the staff are friendly
and helpful. It is open from 6am
to 11am only. Non-dieters should
opt for French toast stuffed with
cream cheese and topped with a
chunky mango or cinnamon
syrup, or blueberry pancakes.
Omelette lovers can select from
any number of combinations
including a Greek inspired feta
and spinach eye-opener. Delicious
home-made bagels, coffee and
juices are all available.
(Inexpensive)

Cafe Roma
Tel: 340-776-6524

Cafe Roma, with its elevated
view of Kogen's Gade, serves
some of the best Italian food on
the island. Owner/chef Josh
Crosley makes everything to
order and produces some
vibrant, punchy flavoursome
dishes. Her sensational fish soup
prepared with garlic butter,
chunks of fresh fish, tomatoes,
and clams in their own broth is
second to none, as is the chicken
or veal piccata served with

fragrant angel hair pasta or tasty seafood dishes served in local spices and herbs. The staff are delightful and diners can be assured of being treated more as honoured friends that customers. Reservations advisable in season. Closed on Tuesday (*Moderate*)

Paradiso Restaurant –
Mongoose Junction
Tel: 340-693-8899

This romantic air-conditioned restaurant serves delicious food that whilst being American-inspired, draws on flavours from around the globe to produce some fabulous cross-cultural combinations. The ever-changing daily specials are determined by what fresh fish and produce has been delivered each morning. The fish dishes are first rate and include warm, rare-cooked tuna coated in black pepper and served with fresh snow peas; broiled mahi-mahi served in orange and lime dressing, or tender beef tenderloin infused with fragrant spices. Open evenings only. (*Expensive*)

Top: The dining room at Asolare on St. John affords magnificent views over Cruz Bay. Centre: Miss Vie in her Snack Shack on St. John. Bottom: Paradiso Restaurant in Mongoose Junction.

Asolare
Tel: 340-779-4747

Asolare sits on a stunning cliff-top setting overlooking Cruz Ba and St. Thomas. This is a magic setting to watch the sun set ar enjoy some of the finest cuisine on the island. The cooking is essentially gourmet Asian Rim and the extensive menu include some refined and technically excellent dishes. Try the tower marinated tuna and salmon, or sautéed frogs legs flavoured w wasabi. An inventory of modish ingredients includes fresh chilli tamarind peanut sauce and coriander dressing. Everything superbly-presented and the management have successfully set an impressive standard wh is reflected in the stylish decor and splendid cooking. Open evenings only. (*Expensive*)

Vie's Snack Shop –
Hansen Bay on the East Road past Haulover Bay.
Tel: 340-693-5033.

Vie is a charming lady whose family has lived on this end of S John since the late 1700s. She has been running her rustic sta for 20 years and cooks up som of the best garlic-fried chicken imaginable. Order at the counte and wait at a shady picnic table

ile she works her magic on
der conch fritters or spicy
at pates.

Tapa
340-693-7755.

cated in Cruz Bay, this
nfortable open-air restaurant
ers an eclectic ever-changing
nu. Owner and chef Alexandra
ald makes her decisions for
menu each morning which
ays includes a tasty selection
capas for lighter snacks.
ditional choices might include a
gonzola Caesar salad served
h a green apple salsa; shrimp
chette with a flawless lime
ssing or a terrific spicy
pacho. Entrées include locally-
ght rare tuna served with a
sted red pepper aioli, or a
bination of grilled chicken,
aragus and shiitake
shrooms sautéed in white-
e and basil sauce served over
sh penne. Excellent service
a fine selection of wines
ke return visits to this spot a
st. Closed on Sunday.
oderate to Expensive)

Chateau de Bordeaux
340-776-6611

s enchanting
taurant sits high
ove Coral Bay in
Bordeaux

Mountain. The setting and
ambience is unsurpassed and
makes a striking impact on
newcomers. The chef has
devised an excellent menu which
is a blend of modern European,
Mediterranean and Caribbean.
Intensely-flavoured dishes include
a succulent rosemary-infused
rack of lamb with a honey
mustard nut crust; a robust
Caribbean gumbo flavoured with
fresh chilli and packed with the
freshest of shellfish; or
chargrilled scallops served with a
wasabi glaze. An excellent
selection of wines are reasonably
priced. Reservations are
essential. Closed for lunch.
(*Expensive*)

ST. CROIX

Top Hat
Tel: 340-773-2346

Located on Company Street, this
authentic wooden-clad
restaurant serves delicious
international cuisine combined
with selection of Danish
specialities including *frikadeller* –
pork and beef
meatballs

served in a zesty tomato sauce,
tender steaks in a creamy
peppercorn sauce and deep-fried
Camembert with loganberries.
Other Danish delights include
herrings in sour cream, duck liver
paté and succulent roast duck
stuffed with prunes and apple.
Closed between May and August.
Open for dinner only. (*Moderate
to Expensive*)

Indies
Tel: 340-692-9440

This attractive courtyard
establishment is packed with
tropical foliage and serves some
of the tastiest food in the area.
The menu has a strong Caribbean
influence and takes its inspiration
from locally-grown herbs, spices
and fruits. Hearty home-made
soups, imaginative salads and
sparklingly-fresh seafood give
this restaurant its well-deserved
reputation. The sushi bar is the
only one of its kind on the island
and is open on Wednesday and
Friday evenings. Open for lunch
Monday to Friday and dinner
seven nights a week. (*Moderate
to Expensive*)

T he US Virgin Islands offer visitors a fabulous selection of magnificent places to enj their vacation ranging from cos intimate inns to luxury five-sta resorts. There is also a wide choice of rental villas, houses o apartments on the islands, as well as National Park campgrounds on St. John.

ACCOMMODATION ON ST. THOMAS

If you are planning to stay on S Thomas, it is worth taking into account whether you want to spend most of your stay relaxin on the beach or meandering through the world-class shoppi opportunities in Charlotte Ama Most of the island's finest restaurants are close to Charlo Amalie, so this should also be another consideration when making your travel plans.

Marriott's Frenchman's Reef a Morning Star
Tel: 340-776-8500
Fax: 340-774-6249

These two properties, both sitting within one resort, have recently undergone a US$50 million renovation and offer a fabulous range of facilities.

Frenchman's Reef is a large ho perched on the edge of a cliff

ang your hat

erlooking Charlotte Amalie.
ost of the rooms have sea
ws and all are spacious and
y furnished in tropical designs
keeping with their
rroundings. The pool complex
erlooks the harbour and
atures waterfalls, fountains, a
uzzi and swim-up bar. There
e also duty-free shops, a state-
the-art fitness centre and
alth spa within this lavish
mplex. The spa provides a
riety of excellent treatments
luding soothing massages and
cial treatments.

e watersports centre offers
orkelling, sailing and parasailing
d diving trips can also be
anged to dive sites in the area.

e Morning Star Resort is
uated directly on the beach
d has 96 rooms housed in a
ries of buildings that line the
ter's edge. They are all
corated in bright colours with
lconies or terraces that afford
her ocean or garden views.
ere is a pool at the end of the
ach, as well as two
staurants and a bar.

e entire complex offers the
oice of five restaurants
luding one that serves
cellent Mediterranean cuisine.
ere are also eight bars.

Hotel 1829
Tel: 340-776-1829
Fax: 340-776-4313

This elegant stone and stucco
building was built by a French sea
captain in 1829 and has operated
as a hotel for over 60 years. It
has been wonderfully restored,
retaining much of its Old World
appeal, and the style is typically
19th-century Mediterranean. This
is particularly evident in the
original 200-year old Moorish
tiling found in the interior
courtyard and in the bar.

Guests enter the hotel up a flight
of ageing brick steps and through
two magnificent carved wooden
doors that lead onto a veranda

and the alfresco dining terrace.
Fifteen rooms, which all vary in
size and décor, are connected by
a maze of walkways, stairs and
courtyards. Various terraces lead
up the hill behind the hotel to a
tiny splash pool, museum and
comfortable seating areas. The
high-ceilinged suites with hand-
hewn wooden beams feature
attractive rattan furnishings.
Whilst they all reflect the historic
character of the property,
modern appliances blend
tastefully and include television,
air-conditioning, ceiling fans and
direct-dial telephones.

*Left: The living rooms at Gallow's Point on
St. John afford stunning sea views. Below:
Frenchman's Reef and Morningstar Resort.*

There is an excellent restaurant and handsome bar equipped with backgammon tables – Vernon Von Boll, the owner, is a world-class champion – on the ground floor. A charming dining room, ideal for private parties, is furnished with elegant antiques, stained glass and Tiffany lamps.

Pavilions and Pools
Tel: 340-775-6110
Fax: 340-775-6110

Located at the eastern end of St. Thomas, a short distance from Red Hook, this delightful complex of private apartments, each with its own private pool, offers total seclusion and relaxation. The resort consists of 25 suites that fan out from a central office building. An honour bar is open from 8am to 9pm and continental breakfast is served here daily. Simple dinners, including barbecues, are served in the dining area most evenings.

Each apartment is air-conditioned and has a full kitchen, living room, dining area and private bedroom. All rooms also have a television and video recorder. The large bathroom and dressing room is reminiscent of a tropical garden

Top: The Renaissance Grand Beach Resort on St. Thomas. Centre: The elegant Ritz Carlton Hotel. Bottom: Fun in the sun at the Sapphire Beach Resort.

and a daily housekeeping servic ensures the perfect break from mundane routine.

Each pool is surrounded by a walled terrace meaning that guests are esconced in their ow private haven and can be sure t achieve a perfect all-over tan in total privacy! The pools are situated right outside the living and bedroom area and sliding glass doors open up to the pool so guests can step directly into the water from either room.

Pavilions and Pools is a ten-minute walk from the beach and some 20-minutes walk from Re Hook. It may be necessary to rent a car during your stay if yo are planning to explore the islan or else stock up on plenty of foo and drinks and go into hiding in your own luxury fortress.

Renaissance Grand Beach Reso
Tel: 340-775-1510
Fax: 340-775-2185

This 290-room resort is situated on the north-eastern coast of S Thomas amidst magnificent landscaped gardens that lead down to a long white sandy beach. The spacious rooms are air-conditioned and have balconies that look out to St. Thomas and the British Virgin Islands beyond.

he watersports centre offers jet
.is, windsurfers and snorkelling
quipment and there is also a
ve centre located on the beach.

he resort also includes a
airdressing salon, fitness centre,
eauty salon, a selection of
ops and a small liquor store.

here are three restaurants that
fer everything from fine dining
 lighter fare and three bars
rving a splendid array of
opical cocktails and fine wines.

tz Carlton
l: 340-775-3333
x: 340-775-4444

n elegant flower-lined driveway
ads to this Italianate palazzo-
yle resort which must be one of
e most magnificent places to
ay in the entire Caribbean.
om the reception area, guests
e afforded an august view
own across sweeping
anicured lawns and sparkling
untains towards the pool and
each. The public areas feature
ystal chandeliers, ornate
ooden furniture and an
nchanting *trompe l'oeil*.

he bedrooms are exquisite and
ave private balconies adorned
th exotic blooms. They are all
-conditioned and have a mini-
ar, television and telephones.

Facilities include tennis courts, a
fitness centre and spa, snorkelling
and windsurfing. Deep-sea fishing
and diving trips can also be
arranged, as well as sunset trips
on the hotel's 53 foot (16-metre)
catamaran. The pool with its
disappearing edge is fabulous and
looks out towards the British
Virgin Islands.

Sapphire Beach Resort and Marina
Tel: 340-775-6100
Fax: 340-775-2403

This hotel is situated on a fabulous
stretch of beach that curves in a
gentle arc around a sandy bay.
This is a great place to stay and
offers endless opportunities for
recreation and relaxation.

All the 171 rooms are comfortable
and include a spacious bedroom,
well-equipped bathroom, living
room with sleeper sofa, dining
table and a small kitchen fitted
along one wall. They are air-
conditioned and have a television
and telephone. The balconies
overlook the beach and the British
Virgin Islands beyond.

There is a stunning two-tier pool
at the end of the beach and a
watersports centre that offers
deep-sea fishing, sailing trips and
scuba-diving, as well as
complimentary snorkelling, sunfish
sailing and windsurfing.

Elysian Beach Resort
Tel: 340-775-1000
Fax: 340-776-0910

This lovely pink-washed resort is
located in 8 acres (3 hectares) of
tropical gardens on a steep
hillside that leads down to a
charming stretch of beach. The
180 rooms and suites overlook
the grounds and the pretty
harbour of Red Hook.

The rooms are bright and
comfortable with rattan furniture
and pastel-toned walls. They all
have wide terraces providing an
ideal place to relax in total
privacy. The larger suites are
equipped with full kitchens and
some are split-level with a
bedroom loft and a second
private balcony reached up a
white spiral staircase. All have
air-conditioning, ceiling fans,
televisions and VCRs.

There is a free-form pool with a
sparkling waterfall directly beside
the beach, and the watersports
centre offers sea kayaks, pedal
boats, floats, snorkelling and
sunfish sailing. Scuba diving,
parasailing, sport fishing trips
and sailing can also be arranged.
There is a state-of-the-art fitness
centre and health club, a tennis
court and a well-stocked
boutique within the complex.

:COMMODATION ON ST. JOHN

ere are some wonderful places
stay on St. John ranging from
l-service five-star resorts to
kury villas or rustic
mpgrounds. The majority of
commodation is found in rental
uses that vary from modest
ices with simple furnishings to
egant homes with a pool,
ectacular views and maid
rvice. Beachfront houses are
ailable, but are less private
an those situated in the hills.

la Aerie

e of the finest and most
mantic places to stay on St.
hn is Villa Aerie which was
nd-built over a six year period
artist Kat Sowa. This
lightful "dolls house" is
rched on one of the highest
aks on the island and is the
ost captivating place anyone
eking total privacy in a perfect
cation could wish to find.

e story behind its construction
quite enchanting as everything
the property was personally
nd-built by Kat. During its
nstruction, she drew on her
perience as an architect, as
ell as an artist, and has
ccessfully created an
chitectural dream in this lovely
me and grounds.

Kat hand-carved all the
woodwork, installed the plumbing
and electricity, lovingly designed
and painted each room in
dazzling colours and equipped the
house with quaint furniture and
artworks. She has included
fabulous antiques such as carved
doors from Haiti, teak armoires
from Bali, as well as leaded glass
and original paintings.

During the building work, Kat
ordered that no tree should be
felled – hence the trees and flora
found growing in unusual places
throughout the grounds. The
paths and walls around the
house incorporate thousands of
shells and are the breathtaking
result of Kat's twelve-year
dedication to beachcombing.

A loft bedroom is reached up a
ladder from the main living room
and affords fantastic views down
to Coral Bay and across to
Tortola. The main bedroom is in a
separate wing and is reminiscent
of a large captain's cabin aboard
an ancient galleon.

The kitchen is equipped with top
quality appliances and is situated
beside a spacious deck. Other
delights include a large open-air
shower and a small plunge pool
on a shady terrace. For details
Tel: Kat Sowa 340-779-4183

Villa rental companies include
Park Isle Villas, telephone: 340-
693-8261. Speak to Mary
Hildebrand, the owner of this
agency who is a mine of useful
information on everything
relating to St. John including villa
rental, sailing, best beaches or
just life on the islands. Her email
address is parkvillas@islands.vi.

Also try Catered To Incorporated,
Telephone: 340-776-6641, Fax:
340-693-8191 or Caribbean Villas
and Resorts, Telephone: 340-776-
6152, Fax: 340-779-4044. Both
companies represent the owners
of dozens of villas located around
the island.

Caneel Bay
Tel: 340-776-6111
Fax: 340-693-8280

Caneel Bay sits on a 170-acre (70
hectare) peninsula edged with a
choice of seven spectacular
sandy beaches, all of which are
very private because most of the
property is only accessible to
hotel guests. The gardens are
magnificent and abound with
glorious tropical flora.

In 1952, a small hotel was
established here by Laurance
Rockefeller on the site of the

*Left: The romantic villa of Aerie on St. John
is the perfect place to escape from reality.*

former Durloo Sugar Plantation. Many of the old buildings still stand in the grounds – most overgrown with a dazzling profusion of exotic flora. Over the years, the property has remained a leader in resort development in the Caribbean and today is a fine example of understated luxury.

The 166 stone-wall bedrooms are beautifully decorated in a comfortable and relaxing style with mahogany four-poster beds and furnishings. Although there is no air-conditioning, ceiling fans and louvered windows keep the rooms cool, and sliding doors open onto terraces that overlook the sands that fringe this resort. This is the place to escape from reality – there are no televisions or telephones in the bedrooms, the

bathrooms feature open-air showers and the guest rooms are dotted throughout the grounds.

Stone paths lead throughout the property to the beaches, restaurants and 11 tennis courts. There are four restaurants in the complex, as well as a bar and a pool. The seven beaches offer excellent snorkelling and guests enjoy complimentary use of sunfish sailboats, kayaks, windsurfing and snorkelling equipment. There is also a fitness centre. The fabulous Turtle Bay Restaurant must be one of the most romantic settings in the world where the sunset views are unsurpassed. The cuisine is nouvelle Caribbean with a distinct American flavour, and the service is gracious and elegant.

Gallows Point Suite Resort

Tel: 340-776-6434
Fax: 340-776-6080

Gallows Point, set just to the south of Cruz Bay, is a collection of fourteen striking two-storey quadraplex condominiums that offer some of the most comfortable accommodation in the US Virgin Islands. All the units hug the rocky shore of this tiny peninsula and have a fully-equipped open-plan kitchen, bedroom, living room with pull-out sleeper sofa and dining area. Each unit contains two garden suites downstairs and two loft suites upstairs. Those situated on the upper floors feature a fabulous cathedral ceiling with a mezzanine bedroom that overlooks the living room. They all have wonderful views of the bay or the open sea.

The complex is immaculate and maintained by an excellent management team who regularly inspect each unit to ensure everything is in working order and sparkling clean. The owners of each condo have added many homely touches including a library of books, CDs and video tapes, as well as "guests logs" for visitors to record their comments of restaurants in the area, the beaches, trails and

htseeing experiences. They all
ve ceiling fans, daily maid
vice and a spacious terrace.

ere is a tiny beach that offers
cellent snorkelling – although it
vise to keep an ear open for
at traffic as the area is quite
sy. There is also a small pool
amidst beautiful grounds
nted with flowering shrubs
m around the Caribbean.

ngton's restaurant offers one
the best views on the island to
tch the sun set over St.
omas whilst sipping cocktails
d enjoying fine cuisine.

cated on the property, St. John
ventures Unlimited, is a
mplimentary concierge service
ere staff provide information
d make bookings for
erything that St. John has to
er. The knowledgeable staff
make dinner reservations
ey keep copies of menus of all
taurants on the island),
ange taxis, organise sailboat
arters, horse riding, car hire
d can advise on any other
vice on the island.

s is a truly perfect base from
ich to enjoy all the treasures
t St. John has to offer before
urning at the end of each day
a peaceful sanctuary in a
ightful setting.

Harmony Camp
Tel: 340-776-6240
Fax: 340-776-6504

Situated on the north shore of St.
John, these 12 two-storey duplex
units are built entirely from
recycled plastics and other
materials. The roofs are made
from recycled cardboard and the
walls were once newspapers! The
entire complex operates on solar
and wind power and all the airy
units are remarkably comfortable.
The top floor rooms are studios
with a cathedral ceiling and the
lower floors have a separate
bedroom area.

The beautiful beach of Maho Bay
is a short walk down the hill and
the views from the complex are
quite magnificent.

Maho Bay Camp
Tel: 340-776-6240
Fax: 340-776-6504

This camp is situated in the hills
above Maho Bay and is adjacent
to Harmony Camp. It has 114
tented cottages all equipped with
two narrow beds, a mosquito net,
a three-burner propane stove and

*Left: The relaxing poolside area at Gallow's
Point on St. John. Below: Harmony Camp
on St. John is constructed entirely from
recycled plastics and materials.*

an ice chest. A couch in the kitchen area converts into an additional bed. There are five centrally-located outhouses and showers which have been adapted to be conscious of wat conservation.

This camp, along with its sister camp, Harmony, is the brainchil of ecological ace Stanley Seleng who has developed several camps for tourism, all designed with an eye for minimal disruption of the environment. Materials are recycled, buildings are constructed on stilts to avoi soil erosion and no roads were bulldozed into the site during construction. The facilities are linked by boardwalks and water piping and electric cables are attached to the underside of the walks to avoid trenching.

There is a small store that carrie a selection of basic provisions, a well as a restaurant and public barbecue area.

Sunfish sailboats, snorkelling equipment and windsurfers are available and diving trips, sailing excursions and hikes can be arranged through the campground staff.

Left: The Westin Resort on St. John sits o a magnificent stretch of beach. Opposite: An alternative form of accommodation!

estin Resort
l: 340-693-8000
x: 340-779-4500

e Westin Resort sits on a wide
c of white sands in 47 acres
9 hectares) of verdant grounds
st a short drive from Cruz Bay.
is is one of the largest resorts
the US Virgin Islands with 285
oms and 96 vacation villas. It
s the largest swimming pool in
e islands, as well as 10,000
uare feet of conference
cilities. The accommodation
its, with their purple roofs, fan
t around the property from a
ntral reception area and are
parated by well-tended lawns,
lms and flower beds.

e resort is primarily aimed at
milies with children and there is
complete child care programme
ailable. This includes
bysitting during the day at no
arge and during the evening at
5$10 per hour. Children can
rticipate in numerous activities
at range from learning about
fferent aspects of island life,
each activities and sports. The
each holds many attractions for
ildren including a huge
flatable slide, kayaks,
ndsurfers and snorkelling.
ere is a daily room charge of
5$10 for the use of all
atersports equipment.

The air-conditioned rooms are
comfortably furnished and blend
West Indian accents with
mahogany woodwork. All have
balconies or patios, dual-line
telephones with voice mail, data
ports for computers, fax and
Internet hook up. A television,
mini-bar and coffee maker are
standard in all rooms.

There are three restaurants and
three bars within the complex,
tennis courts and gift shops.

Cinammon Bay Campground
Tel: 340-776-6330
Fax: 340-776-6458

This campground is located in the
Virgin Islands National Park and is
situated on a fabulous stretch of
white sandy beach.

There are three
types of
accommodation
which include
"cottages" with
two concrete walls
and two screened
walls to allow for
air circulation. They
come equipped
with four narrow
beds, linens, a
table and four
chairs, electric
lights, a ceiling fan,
propane gas

cooker, ice chest and kitchen
utensils. Each has a small patio
with a picnic table and hibachi grill
outside. A cheaper version is the
non-electric tents that come with
virtually the same furnishings.
There are also bare sites that
hold one large or two small tents.

The bathrooms are nearby and
serve both cottage and tent
guests. There is a well-stocked
store in the grounds and
breakfast and lunch are served at
a snack bar near the beach.

The excellent watersports centre
rents windsurfing equipment and
kayaks, as well as scuba and
snorkelling gear. They also
arrange sailing excursions.
(See Get Beached page 73).

ACCOMMODATION ON ST. CROIX

St. Croix is an unspoiled paradise that offers visitors a diverse and interesting holiday destination without being overdeveloped, hurried or commercial. The main town of Christiansted houses a number of historic buildings and it is one of the most attractive towns in the region. There are many pretty beaches and few large resorts which guarantees the holidaymaker serenity and solitude away from the crowds and bustle of St. Thomas.

Above: The Caramabola Beach Resort and Golf Club on the north coast of St. Croix. Opposite: Sprat Hall Plantation is the oldest Great House on St. Croix.

Buccaneer Hotel
Tel: 340-255-3881
Fax: 340-773-2100

This charming property was first opened by the Armstrong family in 1948 and over the years the family have lovingly expanded the facilities to produce the fabulous resort it is today.

The Buccaneer is set on a 240-acre (97 hectare) estate close to Christiansted where reminders of the property's former plantation era days include a sugar mill and remnants of an old manor house. Today the grounds include an 18-hole golf-course, eight tennis courts, riding stables and two swimming pools – one of which sits right on the beach.

There are three beaches within the complex and a watersports centre that offers windsurfing, snorkelling, scuba diving, sailing and fishing. There is also a fitness centre and spa that provides superb massages and other beauty treatments.

The bedrooms range from standard rooms to luxurious deluxe suites. All provide comfortable accommodation, although the ocean-view deluxe rooms set on the hillside afford the best views. There are also cottage suites that sleep up to four people, as well as grand bedrooms in the main building.

Each room is equipped with a refrigerator, telephone, air-conditioning, ceiling fan and television. The restaurants in the complex are all excellent.

Carambola Beach Resort and Golf Club
Tel: 340-778-3800
Fax: 340-778-1682

The Carambola is set in verdant grounds beside a fabulous beach that offers great snorkelling. It features a Robert Trent Jones designed golf course, tennis courts and excellent facilities.

bedrooms are a masterpiece
design and craftsmanship and
cessfully combine Danish
nial reproduction furniture
h modern facilities. They have
ge comfortable sitting areas, a
acious balcony, air-conditioning,
ing fans, direct-dial telephone
d a television.

ere is a large pool situated
ectly on the beach, as well as a
at café/bar which serves tasty
cks and cocktails throughout
e day.

rmorant Beach Club
: 340-778-8920
x: 340-778-9218

s comfortable little inn sits on
abulous stretch of beach and
rs a choice of bedrooms or
dominium units with up to
ee comfortable bedrooms. Its
ximity to Christiansted makes

it an ideal base from which to
explore the island's historic
capital. The pool is situated right
beside the beach and the stretch
of water that fronts the property
offers great snorkelling amidst its
living reef teeming with myriad
colourful fish.

All the spacious bedrooms are
furnished in rattan and decorated
in bright tropical tones. They all
have ceiling fans, air-conditioning,
large bathrooms, and a large
balcony equipped with
comfortable sun loungers.

The ambience of the property is
one of serenity and relaxation.

Sprat Hall Plantation
Tel: 340-772-0305

Sprat Hall is the oldest Great
House on St. Croix and dates
back to the French occupation of
the island between 1650 and
1690. It is furnished with
fabulous mahogany antiques,
many of which date back to the
17th century. A stay on the
plantation makes a wonderful
change from a traditional resort
vacation. There are just 12 rooms
and suites and dinner is served in
a majestic candlelit dining room.
The rooms are air-conditioned
and equipped with a television
and period furniture.

the nitty gritty

planning your trip

how to get there; fare information; tour operators; when to go; what to pack; vaccination and immunisation; visa/immigration requirements; airline essentials & comfort

on arrival

airports; airport taxes

getting around

by air; by bus; by bus; by car

getting acclimatized

climate; business hours; courtesy & respect; electricity; media; money; post & couriers; religion; telephone; time; tipping; what to buy; what to wear

staying alive

health requirements; travel assistance and insurance; beat the heat; tropical diseases and cautions; personal security & safety; emergencies; hospitals; dentists; embassies and consultates

tourist information

US Virgin Islands tourist board and tourist offices overseas

Discovered by Columbus on his second voyage in 1493, the U Virgin Islands lie at the north-west corner of the Lesser Antille to the east of Puerto Rico. Originally inhabited by native Indi tribes, the islands were settled over the centuries by the Dutch, the British, the French, the Spani and finally the Danish.

In 1917, seeking a naval bastion secure access to the Panama Canal, the United States purchas St. Thomas, St. John and St. Cro from the Danes and the islands become an unincorporated territo of the United States. The islande enjoy all the privileges of America citizenship, but are not yet fully enfranchised in government elections and elect only one Representative in the US Senate.

In recent years the economy of t US Virgin Islands, which was larg based on agriculture and sugar cane for over 200 years, has changed completely and tourism now the major source of revenue for the islands. The islands have become one of the most popular destinations in the West Indies, particularly for holiday-makers fro North America who can enjoy a holiday in a tropical environment without any problems of languag currency, immigration formalities and so forth.

English is spoken everywhere – often with an attractive Creole lil The US dollar is the currency; the

no immigration restrictions and
cks are set to Atlantic Standard
e, four hours behind GMT and
hour ahead of Eastern
ndard Time. One reminder of
early British influence is
icles driving on the left-hand
e of the road, but as they are
gely imported from the mainland,
y are also left-handed!

waters offers fantastic
portunities for all types of
tersports and each island has
ny well-researched and
eloped points for snorkelling,
ba and deeper-water diving.
white sand beaches are some
he best in the whole of the
t Indies – all basking under blue
es and bright sun.

landlubbers the US Virgin
nds also claim to offer some of
best duty-free shopping in the
rld. No sales tax, no luxury
es and no customs duties
arantee a paradise for all
pping requirements.

three main islands are
harkably different from each
er. St. Thomas is the most
eloped, and its main town of
arlotte Amalie is the historic
ital of the US Virgin Islands. St.
n, smallest of the three, is the
t developed and is the home of
Virgin Islands National Park. St.
ix is the largest and most
therly island in the group and
some 75 miles (120 km) south
t. Thomas.

planning your trip

How to Get There

Only St. Thomas and St. Croix have international airports; St. John is reached from St. Thomas on the scheduled ferry trips that leave from Charlotte Amalie or Red Hook to Cruz Bay.

At present there are no direct scheduled flights from the UK to the US Virgin Islands; connections have to be made either at a US airport or via another Caribbean island. Charter flights are available and are often good value. A newly-established direct charter flight from London is operated on a once-a-week basis by Caledonian Airways.

British Airways, Virgin Atlantic, American Airlines and Delta offer scheduled services from the UK to various hubs in North America for onward connections.

In North America, US Air fly direct to St. Thomas and St. Croix from Philadelphia and Charlotte and have connections from many other cities across the continent. BWIA and American Airlines fly direct from New York and Miami; Air Canada flies from Toronto and Montreal; Air Jamaica from New York. American Eagle also flies to the islands via its Puerto Rico hub in San Juan. There are many competitively priced connections from many of the other Caribbean islands, flying with Air Carib, Air St. Thomas and LIAT.

(See Fare Information below and Tour Operators overleaf).

The US Virgin Islands are extremely well served by the passenger cruise industry, St. Thomas being one of the premier ports in the whole of the Caribbean. The deep-water harbours at Charlotte Amalie in St. Thomas and Frederiksted in St. Croix are frequently filled with ocean-going liners. Smaller boats are able to anchor in Cruz Bay on St. John.

The larger cruise lines include Cunard, Holland America, Norwegian Cruise Lines, Princess Cruises, Royal Caribbean Cruise Line, Royal Cruise Lines, Renaissance Cruises and Seabourn Cruise Line. There are also many independent operators who offer well-serviced and fully-crewed yachting cruises, which include the US Virgin Islands.

Fare Information

In the UK:

American Airlines 0208-5725555
via Miami or New York to St. Thomas and St. Croix

British Airways 0345-222111
to New York, Miami, San Juan or Antigua with onward connections

BWIA 0208 5771100
to San Juan or New York with onward connections

Caledonian Airways/Golden Lion Travel 01293-567800
direct flights to St. Thomas

Delta Airlines 0800-414767
via Atlanta and New York to St. Thomas and St. Croix

Virgin Atlantic   01293-747747
to New York or Miami with onward
connections

In North America:

Air Canada   1-800-776-3000
from Toronto

Air Jamaica   1-800-523-5585

American Airlines   1-800-433-7300
from Miami, New York and San Juan
to St. Thomas and St. Croix

American Trans Air 1-800-382-5892
charter flights in the high season
from Indianapolis

BWIA   1-800-327-7401

Continental   1-800-523-3273

Delta   1-800-221-1212
from Atlanta

Prestige   1-800-299-8784
from Washington DC via Miami

US Air   1-800-842-5374

In the Caribbean

BWIA   787-778-9372
based in San Juan serves St. Croix
and St. Thomas from most other
islands in the West Indies

Carib Air   1-800-891-0212
based in San Juan flies to St. Croix
and St. Thomas

Vieques Air Link   787-863-3020
flies between Puerto Rico and the
British Virgin Islands

LIAT has offices throughout the
entire Caribbean. In St. Thomas dial
340-776-2313 and in St. Croix 340-
778-9930.

In the US Virgin Islands

Seabourne Seaplane Adventures
(340-773-6442; fax 340-777-4502)
operates a regular service between
the Charlotte Amalie Waterfront in
St. Thomas and Christiansted in St.
Croix. It takes less than 20 minutes
and there are several flights a day.
The return fare is approximately
US$115 and the trip is a unique
way to travel between the islands.

There are regular 30-minute flights
with American Eagle (1-800-474-
4884) between St. Thomas and St.
Croix. The round trip costs
approximately $120.

Virgin Island Hydrofoil Services
(340-776-7417) operate a 150-
passenger hydrofoil *Katrun II* from
the Waterfront in Charlotte Amalie
to St. Croix. The trip takes about
90 minutes and costs around
US$50 each way.

Ferry Schedules to St. John

There are regular ferry rides
between Charlotte Amalie or Red
Hook, St. Thomas and Cruz Bay, St.
John. Telephone 340-776-6282 for
further information.

The Charlotte Amalie ferry dock is
on the Waterfront Highway and the
journey takes about 45 minutes.
Ferries leave Charlotte Amalie at
9am, 11am, 1pm, 3pm, 4pm and
5:30pm. Returning from Cruz Bay,
the ferries depart at 7:15am,
9:15am, 11:15am, 1:15pm,
2:15pm, 3:45pm.

The schedule from Red Hook is c
the hour between 8am and
midnight and from Cruz Bay on t
hour between 6am and 11pm. Th
trip takes about 20 minutes.

Tour Operators

Generally the best bet for a
Caribbean holiday is to put yourse
in the hands of a knowledgeable
travel agent, who can find the be
offer to suit your particular
requirements. The best ones sho
know about combining island
hopping side-trips in your main
ticket. Most Caribbean holidays a
sold as packages, offering differe
destinations and resorts with the
main flights included. The followir
are a few tour operators specialis
in the Caribbean, some of whom
put together a personal package
meet your requirements.

In the UK:

American Connections
Tel: 01494-473173
Fax: 01494-473588

British Airways Holidays
Tel: 01293-723161
Fax: 01293-722624

Caribbean Connection
Tel: 01244-355300
Fax: 01244-310255

Caribbean Expressions
Tel: 0207-431-2131
Fax: 0207-431-4221

Caribtours
Tel: 0207-581-3517
Fax: 0207-225-2491

mplete Caribbean
01423-531031
: 01423-536004

ta Vacations
0207-731-3344
: 0207-735-1606

gant Resorts – St. Thomas
01244-897999
: 01244-897990

lequin Worldwide Travel
01708-850300
: 01798-854952

set
0161-236-6657
: 0161-236-6603

th America Travel Service
0113-243-0000
: 0113 243-0919

mas Cook Holidays
01733-418450
: 01733-417784

pical Locations
0208-427-7300
: 0208-427-7400

& Away Holidays
0208-289-5050
: 0208-466-9099

rldwide Journeys
0207-388-2000
: 0207-383-3848

specialist diving holidays
tact:

lequin Worldwide Travel
01708-852780
: 01708-854952

<u>In the US</u>:

American Express Vacations
Telephone toll free: 1-800 241-1700

Caribbean Concepts,
Tel: 516 496-9800
Fax: 516 496-9880

GoGo Tours
Telephone toll free: 1-800-526-0405

Travel Impressions
Telephone toll free: 1-800-284-0044

When To Go

The more popular time to visit is the dry season from December to May – but the climate varies very little throughout the year. The Christmas and New Year period, as well as the American public holiday dates, are very popular and usually booked up well in advance. The average winter temperature is in the mid 70s (25°C) and in summer rises to the upper 80s (30°C). The gentle trade winds off the ocean keep humidity to an acceptable level. Although three quarters of the annual rainfall occurs between June and October, you can be sure that it will be warm all year round.

Like much of the Caribbean, the Virgin Islands may be affected by a hurricane, both directly or by high winds and rain from hurricanes that pass at a distance. Officially, June to November is the season for tropical storms in the Caribbean at large, but September is regarded as the month at greatest risk. (*See Climate, page 151*)

What to pack

Apart from beachwear (for the beach only!), comfortable and lightweight clothing is all you need, with a lightweight jacket or wrap for the occasional cooler evening. Most restaurants and hotels expect visitors to change out of their beach or sportswear for dinner; cool and easy is the dress code. The US Virgin Islands offers a wide variety of activities on the land – not all of them on flat, paved surfaces. If you plan to enjoy any of the many sporting or outdoor activities, remember to take appropriate clothing. Also a good pair of tennis shoes or comfortable closed walking shoes are a must, as are jeans for horseback riding. Keen bird-watchers should pack a small pair of binoculars.

If you are on regular medication, take supplies with you.

As far as photography goes, be self-sufficient. Bring a spare camera battery (or two) and plenty of film. Although film is available on the island, it is not cheap.

Remember to take sunhat, sunglasses, high factor sunscreen, swimsuits, a basic first aid kit (include travel sickness pills, diarrhoea medication and rehydration salts) and plenty of insect repellent. If you wear contact lenses, remember to bring cleaning solutions, as well as a spare set of lenses.

Vaccination and immunisation

Vaccinations are not required unless arriving from an area where a particular disease is endemic; typhoid, poliomyelitis and tetanus are recommended if in doubt. Children's normal vaccinations should be up-to-date. The biggest plague, however, is the mosquito. While there is no malaria on the islands, dengue fever (a flu-like illness with high fever, aches and an irritating rash several days later) is present and is carried by the mosquito. There is no vaccination against the fever – it is advisable to simply try and avoid mosquito bites.

Visa/Immigration Requirements

US immigration regulations apply to the US Virgin Islands, so valid passports – but no visas, for the time being – are needed by British citizens. North American visitors can enter without restriction provided they carry an acceptable form of ID. Visitors from other parts of the world should check current visa requirements with their local United States information office or embassy.

All visitors must carry a valid ticket for their return or onward journey.

Airline essentials and comfort

The general rule is to have a carry-on bag that is small and light, but provides you with all the comforts you need. Always hand carry your passport/visa, airline tickets, traveller's cheques, cash (including some US dollars), credit cards, toiletry kit and reading material. It is also a good idea to have your driver's licence, itinerary, water, camera and film with you. Make a photocopy of your passport and credit cards and keep them in a separate part of your luggage; make sure you know how to cancel your credit cards should they be stolen. And it is advisable to always hand-carry valuables like jewellery.

Customs & Excise

Non-American visitors to the US Virgin Islands are limited to a duty-free allowance of:

200 cigarettes **or**
50 cigars **or** 2 kg of tobacco

One litre of alcohol, in any form

A reasonable amount of perfume

Other items to a total value of US$100

Allowances on leaving the islands depend on the regulations that apply in your destination.

For the UK the duty free limits are:

200 cigarettes **or** 100 cigarillos **or** 50 cigars **or** 250 grams of tobacco

One litre of alcoholic drinks over 22% vol. **or**
two litres of fortified or sparkling wine or other liqueurs **plus**
two litres of still table wine

50 grams of perfume **and** 250 ml of toilet water

UK£145 worth of other goods; keep receipts for proof of purchase price.

Remember: these allowances are adults; anyone under the age of is not entitled to any tobacco or alcohol allowance. It is prohibited import counterfeit items such as watches, CDs and audio equipme into the UK. Plants, either whole as seeds, bulbs or cuttings, etc. prohibited. Most animals and bird are excluded, as are certain prod made from animals such as ivory and reptile leather goods.

For the USA

As the US Virgin Islands are part the United States, the only limit value. This is US$1,200 per perso and can be used every 30 days. family of five people, making two separate visits a month apart, ca take home to the US goods up to the value of $12,000 in the year!

There is an extensive list of prohibited items, including firearms, drugs, obscene publications and pirated copies of copyrighted wo Plants are banned unless an imp permit has been obtained. Meat meat products may be subject to restrictions. Pets must be free fr any disease that can be passed to humans. Vaccination against rabies is not required for dogs ar cats as long as they are arriving from a rabies-free country.

Further detailed information can obtained from the US Customs Service, PO Box 17423, Washingt DC, 10041; or from the US Emba Grosvenor Square, London W1A

arrival

...ril **E. King Airport** on St. Thomas ...he main airport for the US Virgin ...nds. **Henry E. Rohlsen Airport** ...ves St. Croix. St. John does not ...e an airport of its own.

...ril E. King Airport is about 3 miles ...km) from the capital of Charlotte ...malie. Many visitors prefer to take ...axi to their destination rather ...n cope with hire-car details on ...ival and driving off into the ...nknown, on the left-hand side of ...e road! There is a taxi stand at ...e far end of airport building. Take ...e that it is rather a long walk ...m the arrival point for most ...oming flights from Puerto Rico ...d the other islands so keep hand ...ggage to a minimum.

... St. Croix there are taxis at the ...port for the journey to either ...ristiansted, 7 miles (11 km) to ...e north-east, or Frederiksted, 3 ...es (5 km) to the west, or other ...stinations around the island.

...port taxes

...the islands are part of the US, ...y departure tax payable by non-...citizens is usually included in the ...st of the air-ticket. Make sure ...s has been done before you ...ve home. If you plan to visit ...her islands within in the ...ribbean, there may be a ...parture tax payable depending ...your final destination.

getting around

By air

If you are planning on doing any "island hopping", it is worth investing in one of the "hopper" tickets offered by **LIAT**, the largest carrier in the Eastern Caribbean, which flies in and out of both St. Croix and St. Thomas. There is a LIAT office on St. Thomas at Cyril E. King Airport (340-774-2313), which also serves St. Croix.

Other inter-island flights are offered by **Seabourne Seaplane Adventures** (340 773-6442). (See Fare Information, page 145).

American Airlines are based at Cyril E. King Airport, St. Thomas (340-774-6464). Reservations and information for both American Airlines and **American Eagle** can be obtained by telephoning 1-800-474-4884.

Air Center Helicopters in St. Thomas (340-775-7335) can supply helicopters for scenic island tours or island transfers.

By bus

The **VITRAN** bus service operates around St. Thomas (340 774-5678) and St. Croix (340-773-7746). There is a flat rate of 75 cents for journeys in town and US$1 in the countryside. Exact change is required and there are reduced fares for seniors and students.

On St. Thomas, buses operate during the day between 5:30am and 9:30pm. The route leaves from the Market Place in Charlotte Amalie and Red Hook at the eastern end of the island. On St. Croix, there is a regular service between Christiansted and Frederiksted every day between 5:30am and 9:30pm. On both islands there is a regular bus service from the airport to the main towns.

On St. John the VITRAN service runs regularly between Cruz Bay and Salt Pond. They charge US$1 for any stop on route and follow the Centerline Road to Coral Bay and then continue to the terminus at the end of Salt Pond Road. There are a few official stops along the route, but buses will generally pick up anybody who waves them down.

By car

If you like your independence and are happy to navigate around the island, hire a car. Most of the international car rental companies operate in the US Virgin Islands and vehicles cost in the region of US$50-60 per day. Most companies insist on drivers being over 25 years of age and hold a valid driving licence. It is possible to obtain a temporary licence through the rental company if necessary.

Car hire companies on St. Thomas include:

Avis 1-800-331-1084 or 340-774-1468

Budget Rent-a-Car 1-800-527-0700 or 340-776-5774

National Car Rental 340-776-4858

Thrifty Car Rental 340-775-7282

Tri-Island Rent-a-Car
Havensight 340-776-2879 and Red Hook 340-775-1200

Car hire companies on St. Croix include:
Avis 340-778-9355

Budget Rent-a-Car 1-800-527-0700 or 340-778-9636

Hertz 340-778-1402/773-2100

Thrifty Car Rental 340-773-7200

St. Croix Jeep & Honda Rentals
340-773-0161

On St. John, where jeeps or off-road vehicles are the usual rental vehicle for the relatively rough roads and terrain, there is Hertz (1-800 854-3131 or 340-776-6412) and several other island renters. At present there are no scooter or cycle outlets.

There are many other rental companies on all the islands and these are listed in the Yellow Pages. They offer a selection of suitable vehicles, including mini-mokes, which are great fun in the sun. Also look out for inclusive offers in your holiday and flight package. And there may be useful discount vouchers in travel magazines.

If possible, try to arrange a vehicle in advance of your departure, as this is often cheaper. And in the high season you will have the peace of mind knowing a car is waiting for you. Most companies will arrange an airport or hotel pick-up and collection if required.

Driving in all the Virgin Islands, including the US Virgin Islands, is on the left-hand side of the road. Signs are quite good, so it is not that difficult to find your way around, but keep your eyes open for signs pointing towards the more interesting and off-the-beaten-track delights. The speed limit on St. Thomas is 20 mph (32 kph) in town and 30 mph (48 kph) elsewhere. Afternoon rush hour can bring traffic almost to a standstill in town.

On St. Croix, the limit in town is also 20 mph (32 kph), but varies between 35 mph (56 kph) on other roads and up to 55 mph (88 kph) on the Centre Line Highway between Christiansted and Frederiksted. Even though these speeds are not particularly fast, remember to wear a seat belt all the time.

Remember that US law prevails and there are heavy penalties for drinking and driving, as well as illegal parking. Beware of apparently helpful offers (for a small fee) to find you a parking spot – it may not be a legal one!

Petrol stations are open Monday to Saturday from 6:30am to 8pm; a few may be open on Sundays, but most will be closed on public holidays. Petrol is much more expensive than on mainland USA and must be paid for in cash.

By taxi

The taxis do not have meters, but a list of fares around the islands is published in the local papers – *St. Thomas This Week* and *What To Do*. Every driver should carry the list and display it in his cab. They are permitted to charge a slightly reduced additional fare for each passenger, but make sure they do not charge the full fare for each one. In St. Thomas it is customary for the driver to fill up the taxi with passengers before setting off. This also applies at the airports, so if you are looking to get your destination quickly, look for a taxi that is virtually full.

To avoid argument, agree the fare before you set off. On St. Thomas there are several taxi services. If you telephone to book a taxi you will be given the number of the vehicle who will come to get you. This is also the taxi license number which makes for easy identification. Their charges are reasonably cheap and there is a charge for each item of baggage. Waiting time and after midnight trips out-of-town also incur a surcharge.

Taxi drivers do make excellent island guides and their vehicles can be hired by the hour or more. The number for the Taxi Commission in St. Thomas is 340-693-8294.

St. Croix the Taxi Association
s an office at the airport 340-
8-1088. There are taxi stands on
g Street in Christiansted and by
t Frederik in Frederiksted. For
e Taxi Commission on St. Croix
l 340-773-8294.

etting acclimatized

usiness hours

hough store hours do vary, in
neral they are open Monday-
day from 8:30am to 4:30pm;
turdays 8:30am to 4pm. Some
res may close for a lunch-hour
eak. Most are closed on Sunday
less a cruise ship is in harbour. In
vensight Mall, some shops may
ay open until 9pm on Friday
enings. On St. John, Mongoose
nction and Wharfside Village
ops in Cruz Bay are often open
the evening.

nking hours are generally
onday-Thursday from 8am to
m and Friday from 8am to 5pm.
ey are closed on weekends and
idays.

st office hours are Monday-
day from 8am to 4:30pm and
turday from 8am to 12 noon.

mate

e US Virgin Islands' climate,
hough technically tropical, is
al. Daytime temperatures range
m the low 70s (23°C) to the
ddle 80s (28°C). The hottest
e of the year is June through

August when the mercury may get
up to the low 90s (35°C). The
spring months of February to May
are the driest, with probably no
more than a very comfortable 70
per cent humidity.

The wettest months are usually
May and June and September and
October. But even then, the rain is
usually in short, heavy downpours
and the effects quickly dry out
under the warm sun. The annual
average rainfall is about 50 inches
(127 cm), but the humidity is kept
at an acceptable level by the north-
east tradewinds that blow across
the island throughout the year. A
particular bonus is the Caribbean
current which keeps the islands
surrounded by warm water – so
swimming and sea sports are
always a pleasure.

Being in the Tropics, sunrise and
sunset times are fairly constant
throughout the year. In summer,
the sun rises at around 5:30am and
sets around 6:30pm; in winter
sunrise is about an hour later and
sunset an hour earlier.

Like the rest of the Caribbean, the
US Virgin Islands are well within the
hurricane zone. In 1995, two major
hurricanes, Louis and Marilyn,
caused billions of dollars of damage
and killed several people in St.
Thomas and St. Croix.
Reconstruction and re-building
have repaired the worst of the
damage, but work still continues on
several facilities.

The most likely month for a major
hurricane to develop is September,
although the "season" for
hurricanes can run from the
beginning of June through to the
end of November. If you are unlucky
enough to be in the islands when a
hurricane is imminent, follow local
advice on when and where to take
shelter and DO SO. Do not be
foolish enough to think you know
better as tropical storms of any
magnitude are potentially very
dangerous. There is usually enough
notice of any impending storm to
give visitors the chance to leave
the island before weather
conditions deteriorate.

Courtesy and respect

Politeness, respect and good
manners are an integral part of
Caribbean culture in general. And as
this applies to the residents of the
US Virgin Islands in their everyday
life, they expect visitors to their
islands to do the same. A smile and
warm greeting will go a long way.

Swimwear should be confined to
the beach and pool areas. Although
there is one beach on St. John
where nude bathing is unofficially
permitted, there are strict laws
about wearing revealing clothing in
public places. It is considered
insulting and offensive if you fail to
wear proper clothing over your
swimsuit when you leave the beach
or pool. When walking in town, it is
polite for men to wear a shirt, and
ladies wishing to avoid comments

should not wear too-short shorts. Women who are "indecently" dressed – i.e., wearing hot pants, backless tops or showing a bare midriff – may run the risk of unwelcome approaches.

When taking photographs of anybody or a small group of people, it is courteous to ask first. Many people in the Caribbean, especially the elderly, harbour mysterious ideas concerning photographs, believing that they can be used in spells or will "steal their soul".

If you want to negotiate or "discuss" a price, remember that while this is acceptable and sometimes even expected, do not try to drive to hard a deal.

Electricity

As in the rest of the USA, the US Virgin Islands is on 110/120, 60 cycles voltage, so all American appliances can be used. Small UK dual-voltage items will also work satisfactorily; but European appliances require adapters, which hotels should be able to supply.

Media

One newspaper, *The Daily News*, is available on St. Thomas and St. John. It appears every day and the Friday edition contains a weekend section listing of special events as well as a guide to entertainment and places to eat. St. Croix's newspaper is *The Avis* and the free weekly is *St. Croix This Week*. St. John also has the weekly *Tradewinds*.

The *San Juan Star* is available on St. Thomas, as well as the *Virgin Island Daily News* and *The Island Trader*.

Overseas newspapers and magazines are available at some hotels, news-stands and shops, but are heavily surcharged.

Cable television serves the hotels as well as most homes on St. Croix and St. Thomas. The mainland television companies – ABC, CBS, NBC and PBS – are available as well as CNN, HBO and MTV.

There are several AM and FM radio stations available, including the local music station, WIVI.

Money

The official currency is the US dollar (it is also the currency of the British Virgin Islands), so it is therefore advisable to bring American currency with you. Traveller's cheques are accepted in all the tourist areas. Remember, too, that you are in the Caribbean, which has its own dollar currency – however, when anybody in the US Virgin Islands refers to a dollar, they are almost certainly talking about the US dollar. Do make sure you know which currency you are talking about whenever you are negotiating for something!

If you do have to exchange currency, it is better to do it at a bank than at a hotel, where you would get five to 10 per cent less on the exchange rate. Better rates

are also given for cash rather tha traveller's cheques. Remember th you need identification, such as your passport, when you change money. It is a good idea to keep receipts of exchange transaction

Banks

US banking legislation applies throughout the US Virgin Islands. Banking hours are 8:30am to 3pr on weekdays only. Banks are clos on all public holidays. The main banks are:

Banco Popular Puerto Rico

Fort Mylner Shopping Centre, Charlotte Amalie, St. Thomas (34 693-2861). They have branches i Charlotte Amalie (340-693-2815) and Red Hook (340-693-2823), a well as in the Orange Grove Shopping Centre (340-693-2902) and Sunny Isle Shopping Center (340-693-2935) on St. Croix.

Bank of Nova Scotia, (Scotiabank

They have branches throughout ! Thomas and St. Croix and one in Cruz Bay on St. John (340-776-6552). The main branches on St. Thomas are at the Scotia Bank Building, Charlotte Amalie (340-7 1743), the Waterfront in Charlott Amalie (340-777-9383), Havensig Mall (340-776-5880/6950) and Tu Park Mall (340-777-3322). On St. Croix they have branches at 43 K Street, Christiansted (340-773-1013), 520 Strand, Frederiksted (340-772-0880) and Sunshine Ma Frederiksted (340-692-2440).

rclays Bank plc have branches on Thomas in Charlotte Amalie (0-776-5880) and at Havensight ll (340-774-6991).

ase Manhattan Bank NA have anches in St. Thomas on the terfront (340-775-7777) and also St. Croix in Christiansted (340-3-1222).

ibank NA have branches on St. omas on Veterans Drive, Charlotte alie (340-774-4800) and in vensight Mall (340-774-4800).

edit Cards

major credit cards are accepted most of the shops and staurants – in fact, they are nerally preferred by many sinesses to traveller's cheques. ny credit cards will allow you to tain local cash advances. hough there are ATM machines most banks, they can often be t of order, so it is wise to have equate cash with you at all times.

st and couriers

stage rates and services are the me as the US mainland. Airmail st to the UK usually takes tween five and six days. There is nain post office on each of the ee islands.

ere is a **Federal Express** office at e Cyril E. King Airport on St. omas and for delivery or lection arrangements dial St. omas (340-774-3393) or St. Croix 0-778-8180).

The **Virgin Islands Communications Centre – Connections** on St. John (340-776-6922) in Cruz Bay are the local recipient for national and international courier packages.

On St. Thomas, **UPS** have an office at the airport (340-774-4942) and one at the Al Cohens Plaza in Charlotte Amalie (340-776-1700).

Other national and international courier services are listed in the telephone directory.

Religion

Nearly half the population of the US Virgin Islands follow one of the Christian faiths, some 30 per cent being Roman Catholics. There are churches and meeting places for followers of the Baptist, Lutheran, Moravian, Episcopal and Pentecostal beliefs as well as many other religious strands. Judaism and Islam are also represented.

As in the rest of the Caribbean, religion is a very active and public part of the way of life and visitors are welcome to attend services and details of services are published in local newspapers each week. On Sunday mornings colourful family groups in their brightest and finest outfits can be seen in and around their chosen place of worship.

The Yellow Pages of the telephone directory has an extensive list of the many and varied religious establishments on the islands.

Telephone

The islands' telephone system, VITELCO, is operated by TLD of the Virgin Islands. The area code for the US Virgin Islands is 340.

To dial from overseas, remember that it is the same as any other United States area, so dial the access code, then "340" followed by the seven digit number.

Once on the islands, the local telephone rate is 25 cents for a five-minute call. Private switchboards in hotels and offices may make a charge even for toll-free calls and certainly for inter-island and international ones. Direct-dial overseas and inter-island calls are possible. Although the service is not always as reliable as that on the mainland, there is an improving cellular phone system operated by VITELCO, so your mobile phone will work, provided that it is on a world band network.

It is advisable to carry at least two long-distance calling cards such as AT&T, MCI or Sprint. If you have trouble (either technically or with a stubborn hotel operator), ask to be put through to an international operator, who can help you.

There is an AT&T centre at Havensight on St. Thomas and a call service centre at Sub Base at the Crown Bay Marina.

Unless you have money to burn, DON'T place a long-distance call at your hotel in the normal manner, without a calling card – hotels can, and often do, add a surcharge of an alarming size. Phone cards for various amounts can be purchased locally from the telephone offices, the post offices and various stores.

Time

The US Virgin Islands are in the Atlantic Standard Time Zone, four hours behind GMT (five hours behind during Daylight Savings Time). They are one hour ahead of North American Eastern Standard Time. If it is noon in the Virgin Islands, it will be 4pm in London, 5pm in Rome, 11am in New York and 8am in Los Angeles.

Tipping

Where tipping is appropriate, use the mainland standard of 15 per cent. Some all-inclusive hotels ask that no tips should be given: this will be stated in the information provided at check-in or at the hotel's welcome sessions. Taxi drivers will appreciate at least a 10 per cent tip, while 75 cents or a dollar per bag is a good rule of thumb for porters and bellhops.

What to buy

As the US Virgin Islands are a free port and all tourist related items are duty free, shopping is more a question of how much you can carry back to the mainland than how much your can afford! However do remember it is illegal to export many types of coral, particularly "black coral", from anywhere in the Caribbean, including the Virgin Islands. Coral is already much diminished world-wide by pollution and activities of man as the simple touch of a hand or foot can cause serious harm. It is also illegal to remove anything from the seabed.

Tropical design T-shirts and a bottle of rum are obvious souvenirs, but there is also a fantastic selection of attractive local itemson sale. Apart from the many luxury items you will find in St. Thomas and St. Croix, it is worth also considering taking home some of the fabulous works of art or local crafts. Arrangements can be made for shipping the larger, more fragile and expensive items.

What to wear

As the weather is warm all year round because of the tropical climate, summer clothes are the rule; particularly cottons. However, you may need a wrap or sweater during the cooler winter evenings. The general rule for men during the day is casual resort wear unless one is attending any kind of official function, then smarter attire is required. When shopping in town, wear neat shorts or a skirt and a casual top. Swimwear should be reserved for the beach and do not wear it on the street or in town. The same applies to any skimpy clothing. In general, wear cool, light-coloured clothing.

staying alive

Health Requirements

In addition to the details listed under *Vaccination and immunisati* (*see page 148*), hepatitis A and cholera vaccinations are sometim recommended. Although your ow doctor is probably up-to-date on vaccinations required for travel to various parts of the world, the latest information can be obtaine by contacting the **Center for Disease Control** (CDC) Travellers Hotline in the United States Tel: 404-332-4559; Fax: 404-332-456!

The **International Association for Medical Assistance to Travellers** (IAMAT) is another good source f vaccination information to 120 countries. In the USA, contact them on 716-754-4883 and in Canada on 519-836-0102. They c also be faxed in North America or 519-836-3412. In Europe, IAMAT can be contacted by writing to them at 57 Voirets, 1212 Grand-Lancy-Geneva, Switzerland.

Travel Assistance and Insurance

There is nothing worse than havir a medical emergency – or falling il when you are on holiday. It is therefore strongly recommended that you take out sufficient travel insurance to cover potential medical treatment, as well as you financial investment in the holiday

d luggage and contents
placement. Certain
mprehensive policies may also
mburse you for delays due to
eather or flight delays.

eck with your own insurance
mpany to see if they can supply
s either on a short-term or long-
m basis. Travel agents can
nerally arrange something as well,
t it pays to compare prices and
op around. Make sure you read
e fine print and know what your
clusions are. And, importantly,
ce you have taken out the travel
surance, take a copy of the policy
holiday with you.

ere are several well-known
ganisations, which supply medical
licies and holiday insurance
ckages to travellers. One of the
gest is **International SOS
sistance**, who have a global
erral network of some 2,500
edical professionals and
sistance centres staffed around
e clock, 365 days a year. They
ve many offices around the
orld, including Philadelphia Tel:
15) 244-1500 or (1-800) 523-
30 Fax: (215) 244-2227. London
08-744-0033, Madrid and
neva. They also sell medical kits.

ere are comprehensive schemes
fered in the UK by **American
xpress** (01444-239900);
ailfinders** (0207-938-3939) and
rdine's** (0161-228-3742). Based
the States are a few other

companies offering similar
assistance, such as **Travel
Assistance International** (TAI) in
Washington DC (1-800) 821-2828 or
(202) 331-1609; Fax: (202) 331-
1588); **TravMed** in Baltimore (1-800)
732-5309 or (410) 296-5050; Fax:
(410) 825-7523) and **US Assist**, also
in Washington DC (202) 537-7340).

Beat the Heat

Although the US Virgin Islands are
towards the northern end of the
Caribbean, it pays to remember that
they are still in the "Tropics" – the
area that straddles the Equator.

Do not be fooled – although the
cooling trade wind breezes may feel
soothing as you lie on the beach or
by the pool, you are steadily baking –
think lobster. If want to avoid bearing
a striking resemblance to this tasty
crustacean – and experience the pain
and discomfort that is guaranteed to
come with sunburn – it is advisable
to remember a few things:

Ignore the song about mad-dogs
and Englishmen and **avoid** the
midday sun. Make a gentle start on
your tan and give yourself no more
than a half-hour in the sun in the
morning and another half hour in the
late afternoon.

Clouds do NOT protect against UV
rays. You will still get burned if you
are not careful. Look for a high SPF
when choosing your sun lotion – and
try to ensure it really is water-
resistant. If not, reapply after each
time you have been in for a swim.

Remember the water can be a
dangerous mirror reflecting the
sun's harsh rays, so even if you are
sitting beside the pool, or on the
beach, you are experiencing a
double dose of strong sun. The
glare and reflection will also affect
you and can cause severe headaches and feelings of nausea.

Always wear strong sunglasses
and a broad-brimmed hat. Do not
be ashamed to cover up when you
need to! If you are starting to turn
pink today, then it is likely you will
be as red as a beet tomorrow.
Snorkellers, in particular, should
beware of burnt backs: a long T-
shirt – and even lightweight
trousers if need be – will help avoid
the problem.

Water, water and more water. That
means drink it, not just swim in it.
And remember that while you are
swimming, water reflects the rays
of the sun, so even though you
may feel cool, it is likely that you
are still burning. The sun also does
more than burn – it dehydrates. So
drink water as often as possible; a
large glass every 30 minutes to
one hour is recommended. Avoid
sugary drinks and use salt on your
food to rehydrate your system.

The best remedies for sunburn are
either calamine lotion applied to the
skin or aloe, either the gel or sap
straight from the leaf of the plant
or commercial products. A mixture
of two-thirds water and one-third
vinegar, applied to the skin will also

help alleviate discomfort. Take aspirin regularly which will help reduce the inflammation.

Too much sun will often cause heat stroke and you will recognize its onset by the following symptoms. Your skin is red, hot and dry; your body temperature is high; you are confused mentally and you lose co-ordination. If this should occur you should cover yourself in cold wet cloths and occur seek medical help.

Tropical Diseases and Cautions

Dengue fever is carried by the mosquito and can be hard to detect, because its symptoms are similar to flu – high fever, joint pain, headaches and an irritating rash several days later. There is no treatment for this disease, so try to avoid getting bitten. Use tried-and-tested repellents and wear long trousers and long sleeves when the mosquitoes are most prolific at dawn and dusk. If you get the disease, drink plenty of liquids, take *acetaminophen* (not aspirin) and rest for a few days.

Montezuma's Revenge – well, no one wants to talk about it, but many of us get it when we travel to an exotic destination: the dreaded diarrhoea. It is generally caused by viruses, bacteria or parasites contained in contaminated food or water. Use common sense and err on the side of caution. When in doubt about the condition of the

water, used bottled and ensure it is sealed – and avoid ice in drinks: remember, it is made from water!

Make sure hot foods are cooked properly and cold foods have been kept cold. Peel fruit and vegetables before eating them. Avoid eating prepared food from roadside stands unless you are sure it has been kept at constant temperatures.

If you are still unlucky enough to be taken ill, there are a few things you can do. If it is a serious case, seek medical attention immediately. Otherwise, take Pepto Bismol (*bismuth subsalicylate*), which slows down the process, but still lets it run its course. Avoid taking Imodium (*ioperamide*) unless you absolutely have to as it totally blocks up the digestive tract and locks in infections.

The best treatment is rest, plenty of fluids and salt replacement. The best antibiotic for bacterial types of travellers' diarrhoea is *ciproflaxicin*. Take regular small portions of bland fluids – ginger ale, flat cola and salty chicken broth are all effective. Try to avoid getting dehydrated, which can be dangerous, especially for children. It is advisable to carry oral rehydration packets with you.

Venereal disease is prevalent in the Caribbean, as is HIV, so remember the dangers of casual sex. Always check that properly sterilised or disposable needles are used should you require medical attention.

Nature's Nasties

Hiking and camping during the dr season – December through April may bring unpleasant encounters with blackflies and sandflies as w as the ubiquitous mosquito. Spra and repellents are essential, particularly those which are citronella based, and a mosquito net is vital for anyone planning to sleep in one of the campsites, or a house that does not have screens or air-conditioning.

As the mongoose put paid to the poisonous snakes on the island, there is only one creepy-crawly to be avoided. The centipede, with it segmented reddish-brown body and many legs, is the only creatur that can give the unwary visitor a poisonous bite. If you do see one, do not touch it.

Some of the terrestrial flora can b equally unpleasant. Certain trees and plants should be admired only from a safe distance such as the **manchineel** tree, which grows in coastal areas. This is a medium-sized tree with bright green leave Its green fruit resembles crab apples. The entire tree produces sap that causes skin irritation and blistering. Do not touch or eat the apples and do not sit under the tree during a shower, as the rain will wash the sap onto your skin.

The prolific and beautiful **oleander** is often used as a border for gardens and lawns; its usually pin

...wers look much like the ...ountain laurel. The wood from ...s plant is extremely toxic and ...ould not be burned – so if you ...ve any impromptu barbecues, ...oid this willowy plant.

...rine menaces include young **...rtuguese men-of-war**, which ...metimes visit the Atlantic coast ...aches. Generally light blue or ...k in colour, tinged with purple, ...ey appear to be tiny bubbles of ...stic floating in the water, trailing ...ew thready tentacles. They can ...e nasty rope-like stings, which ...e painful but not dangerous. You ...n even get stung if you step on ...e that has been washed up on ...e beach, so tread with care. Tea ...e oil applied directly to the ...ected area offers some relief.

...rsonal Security and Safety
...e your common sense at all times

...e US Virgin Islands have their fair ...are of crime, so keep temptation ...t of the way. Wear discreet ...vellery, lock up your valuables, ...ry little cash, always lock your ...r doors, never wander in ...serted streets or alone on the ...ach at night and keep hold of ...ur purse at all times. Never leave ...ur belongings unattended on the ...ach as it is unlikely they will be ...ere when you return.

...oid threatening areas, such as ...rts, rowdy bars and red-light ...tricts – particularly at night. ...ek local advice on what other

areas to avoid. If you do get robbed, don't try to be a hero just give them what they want and don't pick a fight. Although there have been frightening incidents involving tourists in recent years, don't let that spoil your holiday; if you don't look for trouble, it is unlikely that it will find you.

If you are driving, don't stop even if you are flagged down and never pick up hitch-hikers. Don't let something that is not your problem become your problem. If you are worried about it, call the Emergency Services on 911 from the next available phone.

You will probably encounter street hawkers and peddlers on the beach. Drugs are illegal and an increasing problem on the islands. Marijuana and crack cocaine use is widespread and often distributed on the beaches. Remember that the laws against their use can be punitive. The best rule is a polite, but firm "no thanks", and if they persist or get increasingly obnoxious, remove yourself and find another spot. On the street – just keep on walking!

Emergencies
For **Police**, **Fire** and **Ambulance**: dial 911 (in all three islands)

US Coast Guard for air and sea rescue emergency only: dial 787-729-6770

The police headquarters is 340-778-2211

Hospitals
The main hospital on St. Thomas, with 250 beds, is the **Roy Lester Schneider Hospital** (340-776-8311) in Sugar Estate, Charlotte Amalie.

In St. Croix there is the **Charles Harwood Complex** (340-773-1311), also with 250 beds, and the **Governor Juan F. Luis Hospital** (340-776-6311) on Route 79 just north of the Sunny Isle Shopping Center in Christiansted. There is also the **Ingeborg Nesbitt Clinic** in Frederiksted (340-772-0750).

On St. John, there is the **Morris de Castro Clinic** with 10 beds at Cruz Bay (340-776-6400).

All three operate a 24-hour emergency service. The **Red Hook Family Practice**, which is a walk-in service, is open Monday to Friday between 11am. and 4pm.

Dentists
There are a number of dental surgeries, providing different services including orthodontists, periodontists, endodontists and oral surgery. These are listed in the Yellow Pages of the telephone directory. Hotel reception staff will also be able to advise on the most appropriate one to contact.

Pharmacies
For basic toiletries as well as medicines, try:
Sunrise Pharmacy at Red Hook (340-775-6600)

Havensight Pharmacy in the Havensight Mall (340-776-1235)

People's Drug Store in Christiansted (340-778-7355)

Sunny Isle Shopping Center on St. Croix (340-778-5537)

D & D Apothecary Hall in Frederiksted (340-772-1890)

St. John Drug Center in Cruz Bay (340-776-6353)

Tourist information

St. Thomas: The office for the **Tourism Authority** is in the Elainco Building behind the Post Office on Main Street in Charlotte Amalie (340-774-8784). It is open on weekdays from 8am to 5pm. There is also a **Visitors Hospitality Lounge** (See Sightseeing Spectacular, page 31). There is a **Tourist Information Centre** at the Airport which is open every day between 9am and 7pm.

St. Croix: The **Tourist Information Centre** is on Queen Cross Street, Christiansted (340-773-0495). There is a **Tourism Desk** in the baggage claim area at Alexander Hamilton Airport (340-778-1061). There is also a **Visitors' Bureau** in Christiansted, on Queen's Cross Street (340-773-0495), and Frederiksted, in the Customs House Building on Strand Street (340-772-0357).

St. John: The **Tourism Office** is next to the Post Office at Cruz Bay (340-776-6450).

The Virgin Islands Tourism Offices overseas

London
Molasses House
Clove Hitch Quay
Plantation Wharf
London SW11 3TN
Tel: 0207-978-5262
Fax: 0207-924-3171

Canada
3300 Bloor Street W,
Suite 2120
Centre Tower,
Toronto M8X 2X3
Tel: 416-362-8784
Fax: 416-362-9841

Germany
Postfach 10 02 44
D-6050 Offenbach
Germany
Tel: 069-892-008
Fax: 069-898-892

Italy
Via Gheradini 1
20145 Milan
Tel: 02-33-10-58-41
Fax: 02-33-10-58-27

Denmark
Park Allé 5
DK-8000, Aarhus Center
Tel: 86-181-933
Fax: 86-181-934

USA
1270 Avenue of the Americas
Suite 2108
New York, NY 10020
Tel: 212-332-2222
Fax: 212-332-2223
Toll-free: 1-800-USVI-INFO

Public Holidays in the Virgin Islands

1 January	New Year's Day
6 January	Three Kings Day
15 January	Martin Luther King's Birthday
February	Lincoln's Birthday
31 March	Transfer Day
March/April	Easter
Early April	Sportsweek Festiva St. Croix
Mid April	Rolex Regatta
Late April	St. Thomas Carniva
May	Mumm's Cup Regatta –
1 June	Memorial Day
July 3	Danish West Indies Emancipation Day
July 4	US Independence D
September	Labor Day
1 November	Liberty Day
11 November	Veterans Day
November	US Thanksgiving D
25 December	Christmas Day
26 December	Second Christmas

ndex